ISBN 978-0-932010-04-9   paperback
ISBN 978-0-932010-03-2   electronic book, EPUB
ISBN 978-0-932010-05-6   electronic book, MOBI

Academia Publishing Company
rrsylvester.com

Acknowledgments

The author recognizes the significant suggestions, insights, and thoughtful comments by law professors, attorneys, and hosts for Airbnb and HomeAway. Airbnb host revenue data is from Scott Shatford, www.airdna.com. The back cover photograph is by Kevyn Major Howard. The book illustration and photography is by the author.

Dedicated to The Honorable Dianne Feinstein, United States Senate

Caveat

*The facts and data in this document
are accurate to the extent of the author's knowledge and belief. Within the
scope of the subject, the relevant critical facts and relationships are disclosed.
However, the scope of this document is limited; many related issues and
many details are not discussed.*

*No opinion is rendered on whether
the issues, methods or concepts would be applicable to a specific situation.
Any financial projections presented are hypothetical and may not conform to any
specific situation. Statutes and court interpretations are subject to change. The
reader is cautioned to seek independent, unbiased, specialized counsel for any
specific transaction.*

Table of Contents

Foreword

This treatise is prepared in response to questions raised by federal agencies, city planners and leading attorneys regarding the sharing economy and city ordinances which restrict short term rentals. The current high interest in short term rentals is the result of several factors:

The substantial financial size and rapid growth of internet booking firms, such as Airbnb and HomeAway, and the subsequent major economic benefits to cities resulting from the multiplier effect of tourist and host expenditures.

The unusually stringent terms of the Ordinance passed by the City of Santa Monica on May 12, 2015, which appears to violate fundamental law: California Constitution Article XIII C and U.S. Constitution Fifth Amendment Taking and Substantive Due Process. If a court determines that the Santa Monica restrictive ordinance overreaches, and is therefore deemed to be a taking of property rights, Santa Monica will incur the financial risk of being required to **pay $207 million for just compensation** to property owners.

The Supreme Court decision, *City of Los Angeles v. Patel,* 135 S.Ct. 2443 (2015), which made void a long standing city ordinance which interfered with a fundamental right of the U.S. Constitution.

The false economy of attempting to increase city tax revenue through lodging taxes, which results in lower tourism spending because tourists are sensitive to price. Thus, most of the lodging tax proceeds must be spent on increased tourist advertising, to offset the loss in tourism.

The questionable decisions of the Santa Monica city council which raise issues of possible impropriety of campaign contributions and undue influence from hotel worker unions. Although the city council asserts concern for low-income rentals, the rental restrictions would cause over $5 million reduction in tax revenue, resulting in substantially lower funds available to fund land purchases for low income rentals.

The Critical Issue—Overreaching

A finder of fact could determine that the Santa Monica Ordinance **goes too far,** resulting in a clear violation of the Fifth Amendment Taking Clause and substantive due process guaranteed by the U.S. Constitution. Property is a **bundle of rights**. The bundle of rights may be sliced and diced to the discretion of the owner, as shown by precise segregation of music rights which results in higher income for the owner.

For real property, several centuries of English common law establish that a property owner has a fundamental right to rent without limitation as to duration, whether for 1 day, 30 days, or 99 years. Despite the lack of supporting evidence, city councils assert that short-term rentals cause disruption of neighborhood values. By contrast, the reality is that the environmental and neighborhood effect of a short-term rental guest is comparable to an ordinary visit from a friend or relative. The economic effect of short-term rentals is profound, with sharply higher income for owners, improvements to property, and increased local spending, the result is higher property values for the entire neighborhood and a more prosperous local economy.

For example, in the Venice and Marina area of Los Angeles, an area with many short-term rentals, small homes that sold for $260,000 in 1999 are now selling for $1.2 million. The obvious benefit to the city is <u>vigorous economic growth</u> due to the multiplier effect of spending by the property owners, shopping and restaurant purchases by the international tourists, increase in sales tax income, and higher property tax income after each property is sold.

Calling a home a *de facto* hotel does not make a home a hotel; calling a tail a leg does not make a dog have five legs. Mischaracterization is fraud. To the extent that city ordinances restrict short-term rental income the result is a Taking which requires Just Compensation by the city. The amount of the just compensation is the economic damages caused by the ordinance. For the May 12, 2015 Santa Monica ordinance, calculations demonstrate that the required compensation is **$207 million.**

The wording of the Santa Monica ordinance, by criminalizing ordinary economic behavior, is properly classified as **draconian**, a harsh, unforgiving and severe law with heavy punishments for mere *de minimus*, *de jure* offenses. [1]

For centuries, a residence has protected status against government overreaching. The special status of a home is clearly stated in English Common Law:

> **The poorest man may in his cottage bid defiance to all the forces of the Crown**. It may be frail; its roof may shake; the wind may blow through it; the storm may enter; the rain may enter; **but the King of England cannot enter** - all his force dares not cross the threshold of the ruined tenement! [2]

Risk. The danger of government overreaching is shown by the subtle trend toward **destruction of fundamental values from the inside**, not from a foreign power. As described by Lincoln in his 1838 Lyceum Address which warned of disrespect for fundamental freedoms established by the U.S. Constitution:

> Shall we expect some transatlantic military giant to step the ocean and crush us at a blow? Never! All the armies of Europe, Asia, and Africa combined, with all the treasure of the earth (our own excepted) in their military chest, with a Bonaparte for a commander, could not by force take a drink from the Ohio or make a track on the Blue Ridge in a trial of a thousand years. At what point then is the approach of danger to be expected? I answer. If it ever reach us **it must spring up amongst us**; it cannot come from abroad. **If destruction be our lot we must ourselves be its author and finisher. As a nation of freemen we must live through all time** or die by suicide. [3]

Excessive Government Regulation. In a free economy, the best solutions are derived from innovation, freedom from oppressive regulation, and incentives for continuous improvement in quality and performance. City governments, like the Italian city-states of the Machiavelli era, focused on increasing revenue from taxes and expanding their employment and influence. The result was continuous

---

[1] https://en.wikipedia.org/wiki/Draco_(lawgiver)

[2] Miller v. U.S. (1958), 357 U.S. 301, 307, Justice Brennan citing William Pitt, Earl of Chatham, *Speech on the Excise Bill,* House of Commons (March 1763), as quoted in Lord Brougham, *Historical Sketches of Statesmen Who Flourished in the Time of George III* (1855), I, p. 42.

[3] https://en.wikipedia.org/wiki/Abraham_Lincoln%27s_Lyceum_address

overreaching in unnecessary regulation of activities that should have been left very much alone.

The historical example of excessive regulation is the United Kingdom Locomotive Act of 1865 (the "Red Flag Act") which limited the speed of an automobile to only 4 mph, and required a man carrying a red flag to walk at least 60 yards in front of road vehicles when hauling multiple wagons.[4]

Decline in Court Quality caused by Budget Cuts. The recent economic recession resulted in severe cuts in California court funding which has resulted in questionable court decisions which some now view as precedents. The minimal court budget is noted by the Chief Justice:

> Marking an annual budget clash between California's courts and the other two branches of government, California Supreme Court Chief Justice Tani G. Cantil-Sakauye used her State of the Judiciary speech on Monday to once again urge Sacramento to augment funding for the judiciary. …As California sought to dig itself out of a deep fiscal hole during the recession, the court system was one recipient of wide-ranging budget cuts…."It's not enough. We fall short," Cantil-Sakauye said, with consequences that include "courthouse closures, reduced hours, and employees who are still, yes, on furlough." … "After having the judicial branch suffer over a billion dollars in cuts over five years, we understand the need to innovate and accelerate, and find efficiencies and innovations has to move faster…" [5]

The Importance of Small Changes. The current public resistance to the Santa Monica Ordinance may be viewed as a canary in the coal mine which gives notice of impermissible conditions. The growing concern for city councils to tax and regulate short-term rentals appears to be driven by greed and the drive for power,[6] with no recognition that the regulations and restrictions will damage the income of property owners and the entire local economy.

For Santa Monica, the new ordinance is calculated to cause **$207 million loss of income** for 700 property owners over the next decade. Additional damages are caused to the local economy. Due to the multiplying effect of decreased spending by each recipient, the total economic effect will result in **$728 million damage** to the local economy.

---

[4] https://en.wikipedia.org/wiki/Locomotive_Acts
[5] http://www.sacbee.com/news/politics-government/capitol-alert/article16132724.html
[6] As stated by John E. D. Acton, "Power tends to corrupt, and absolute power corrupts absolutely." http://www.britannica.com/biography/John-Emerich-Edward-Dalberg-Acton-1st-Baron-Acton

It is the <u>slow erosion</u> in minor increments that produces total destruction. It is continuous rust that destroys a steel battleship over three decades. The minor change, termed the difference limen, or the Weber-Fechner law, is the threshold at which a change is perceived. Accordingly, if only minor changes are introduced, the public is unlikely to notice the changes. [7]

History is instructive regarding the cumulative effect of seemingly moderate changes. For example, incremental changes resulted in the Third Reich, based on subtle shifts in laws combined with stringent enforcement over several years:

> …Under pressure from politicians, industrialists, and the business community, President Paul von Hindenburg appointed Hitler as Chancellor of Germany on 30 January 1933. This event is known as the *Machtergreifung* (seizure of power). In the following months, the NSDAP used a process termed *Gleichschaltung* (co-ordination) to rapidly bring all aspects of life under control of the party.
> …In March 1933, the Enabling Act, an amendment to the Weimar Constitution, passed in the Reichstag by a vote of 444 to 94.This amendment allowed Hitler and his cabinet to pass laws—**even laws that violated the constitution**—without the consent of the president or the Reichstag.
> …. Everyone and everything was monitored in Nazi Germany. Inaugurating and legitimising power for the Nazis was thus accomplished by their initial revolutionary activities, then through the improvisation and manipulation of the legal mechanisms available, **through the use of police powers** by the Nazi Party … and finally by the expansion of authority for all state and federal institutions…. [8]

The Future View. Correct decisions require emphasis on prediction of future income and costs, translated into the present value of future cash flow. In error, many decisions are based on historical data and prior decisions instead of the paradigm shifts in circumstances and the necessary focus on <u>future</u> results. For example, it is a fundamental error to drive a car by looking through the rear view mirror. A prior historical decision, with different circumstances, is not a valid precedent. Clearly, it is erroneous to repeat a mistake somehow expecting a

---

[7] https://en.wikipedia.org/wiki/Just-noticeable_difference

[8] https://en.wikipedia.org/wiki/Nazi_Germany

different result. Prudent decisions require focus on foreseeable future events, and the futurity of present decisions.

Approach. This book emphasizes basic objectives, alternatives, the influence of relevant federal law, and feasible approaches. The first step is an accurate *description* of current status, including even unpalatable facts. The next step is a *creative* election of alternative courses of action. Then, detailed discussion and analysis can allow dispassionate review of the foreseeable financial effect of alternative courses of action, based on specific decision criteria. Ethics must provide the essential foundation for selection of the decision criteria.

The basic problem is the failure to correct errors. Mistakes happen. Instead of defending mistakes, the correct approach is continuous improvement [9] based on prompt correction of mistakes. Even seemingly sound management decisions are subject to distortion because of hidden or seemingly minor factors which cause a major change in the result.

With regard to correct design of a city ordinance, the emphasis must be on what is right, not on who is right.[10] Decisions can be improved, based on carefully defined issues, accurate measurement, and abiding by the results of measurement, as contrasted to a confused welter of conflicting opinion.

---

[9] See: W. Edwards Deming, *Out of the Crisis*. Cambridge: The MIT Press, 2000.

[10] As stated by Thomas Huxley, "It is not who is right, but what is right, that is of importance." http://www.brainyquote.com/quotes/quotes/t/thomashuxl152612.html

1. *Discussion of Fifth Amendment Taking*

As shown by recent U.S. Supreme Court decisions, there is increased emphasis on protection of fundamental rights and liberties protected by the U.S. Constitution, with focus on **substantative due process** and **government taking of property rights** which requires just compensation under the Fifth Amendment Taking Clause.

The decisions of the U.S. Supreme Court reflect a variety of approaches which are refined over several decades, and early dissents may later become the foundation for holdings. With regard to whether a specific city ordinance overreaches and goes too far, specific facts and circumstances are reviewed by the Court to determine whether the regulations exceed permissible limits. The primary issues are whether the ordinance is within a specific prohibition of the Constitution, whether the affected persons are insufficiently protected by ordinary political processes,[1] the extent of diminution in property value for a partial taking,[2] and whether the facts indicate excessive, unfair, or unscrupulous exercise of state or city power.

Recent case decisions demonstrate the continuous refinement of the meaning of the Constitution, and whether specific city actions exceed permissible limits.[3] The following is an overview of the basic concepts.

---

[1] See: *U.S. v. Carolene Products*, 304 U.S. 144 153 n. 4 (1938)

[2] The magnitude of the economic impact is viewed as a central factor. See: *Penn Central Transportion v. New York*, 438 U.S. 104 (1978). "...Some values ...must yield to the police power. But obviously the implied limitation must have its limits, or the contract and due process clauses are gone. One fact ... in determination of such limits is the extent of the diminution...while property may be regulated to a certain extent, if regulation goes to far it will be recognized as a taking..." *Pennsylvania Coal Co. v. Mahon*, 260 U.S. 393, 413-415 (1922).

[3] Sequential refinements in decision criteria are shown by *Agins v. City of Tiburon*, 447 U.S. 255 (1980), *Montery v. Del Monte Dunes at Monterey*, 526 U.S. 687, 704 (1999), and *Lingle v Chevron*, 544 U.S. 528, 542 (2005).

Substantive Due Process. *Substantive* due process is a principle used to protect fundamental rights from government interference under the authority of the due process clauses of the Fifth and Fourteenth Amendments, which prohibit the federal and state governments from **depriving any person** of life, liberty, or **property**, without due process of law. [4] By contrast, *procedural* due process is intended to determine whether a person had sufficient notice and the opportunity for a fair and impartial hearing.

Fifth Amendment. The Fifth Amendment Takings Clause requires *just compensation* when a government takes property rights. Although city zoning actions are authorized by the police power, the city <u>overreaches and goes to far</u> when the property owner incurs significant economic loss.

> No person shall be held to answer for a capital, or otherwise infamous crime, unless on a presentment or indictment of a grand jury, except in cases arising in the land or naval forces, or in the militia, when in actual service in time of war or public danger; nor shall any person be subject for the same offense to be twice put in jeopardy of life or limb; nor shall be compelled in any criminal case to be a witness against himself, **nor be deprived of life, liberty, or property, without due process of law; nor shall private property be taken for public use, without just compensation**. *U.S. Constitution, Fifth Amendment.*

Fourth Amendment. Individuals have fundamental **right of privacy.** Without a court order signed by a judge and supported by probable cause, **a state law or city ordinance cannot require** any company or individual to provide information which would allow identification of persons who might be in violation of a law.

> The right of the people to be secure in their persons, houses, papers, and effects, against unreasonable searches and seizures, shall not be violated, and no Warrants shall issue, but upon probable cause, supported by Oath or affirmation, and particularly describing the place to be searched, and the persons or things to be seized. *U.S. Constitution*, Fourth Amendment.

---

[4] See: https://en.wikipedia.org/wiki/Substantive_due_process
Also see: https://www.law.cornell.edu/anncon/html/amdt5bfrag4_user.html

Supremacy. The U.S. Constitution and Federal Statutes are dominant over state or local law. Any state law or city ordinance which conflicts with the U.S. Constitution or federal statutes is void, *ab initio.*

> **...This Constitution, and the Laws of the United States** which shall be made in pursuance thereof; and all treaties made, or which shall be made, under the authority of the United States, **shall be the supreme law of the land; and the judges in every state shall be bound thereby**, anything in the constitution or laws of any state to the contrary notwithstanding.... *U.S. Constitution, Article Six*

Fourteenth Amendment. The Fourteenth Amendment requires the states to honor the fundamental rights granted by the U.S. Constitution.

> All persons born or naturalized in the United States, and subject to the jurisdiction thereof, are citizens of the United States and of the state wherein they reside. **No state shall make or enforce any law which shall abridge the privileges or immunities** of citizens of the United States; **nor shall any state deprive any person of life, liberty, or property, without due process of law**; nor deny to any person within its jurisdiction the equal protection of the laws. U.S. Constitution, *Fourteenth Amendment, Section One*.

Discussion of Property Rights

Property is defined as a <u>bundle of rights</u>, which includes not only the tangible land and improvements, but also the intangible rights, such as the right to rent the property without unreasonable restrictions. The Fifth Amendment term "property" is defined as the entire group of rights owned by a person, such as the right to possess, the right to use, the right to improve, and the right to future income from rental. [5]

---

[5] *United States v. General Motors Corp.*, 323 U.S. 373, 377-78 (1945).

3

The ownership of property rights without unlawful deprivation is essential. As noted by William Blackstone:

> So great moreover is the regard of the law for private property, that it will not authorize the least violation of it; no, not even for the general good of the whole community, William Blackstone, I *Commentaries on the Law of England* 139 (1765). Also see: *Conger v. Pierce County*, 198 P. 377, 379 (Wash. 1921).

This concept is emphasized by James Madison:

> Government is instituted to protect property of every sort .... This being the end of government, that alone is a just government, which impartially secures to every man, whatever is his own. 14 *Papers of James Madison* 266 (Robert A. Rutland et al. eds., 1983).

For several critical cases, the U.S. Supreme Court has recognized overreaching by the exercise of government police power and the critical role of the U.S. Constitution to protect property rights. The takings clause documents the fundamental entitlement of protected status for property rights.[6]

Modern Supreme Court regulatory taking cases often attribute the origin of regulatory taking analysis to Justice Holmes' opinion in the landmark case *Pennsylvania Coal Co. v. Mahon*, 260 U.S. 393, 413 (1922) where Holmes stated that "**if regulation goes too far it will be recognized as taking**."

The police power "must have its limits" and "[w]hen it reaches a certain magnitude, in most if not in all cases there be an exercise of eminent domain and compensation to sustain the act." This point was emphasized in a later case by Justice Brennan:

> Police power regulations such as zoning ordinances and other land-use restrictions can **destroy the use and enjoyment of property in order to promote the pubic good** just as effectively as formal condemnation or physical invasion of property. *San Diego Gas & Elec. Co. v. City of San Diego*. 450 U.S. 621, 652 (1981).

---

[6] Lawrence H. Tribe, *American Constitutional Law* (2d ed. 1988). 608. See: *Lynch v. Household Fin. Corp.*, 405 U.S. 538, 552 (1972). Also see: John Lewis, *A Treatise on the Law of Eminent Domain in the United States* (3rd edition, 1909).

More recently, the Supreme Court expressly reaffirmed this position:

> [l]f . . . the uses of private property were subject to unbridled, uncompensated qualification under the police power, 'the natural tendency of human nature would be to extend the qualification more and more until at last private property disappear[ed], *Lucas v. South Carolina Coastal Council*, 505 U.S. 1003, 1014 (1992) (quoting *Pennsylvania Coal*, 260 U.S. at 415).

The imprecise and highly deferential rational basis standard of *Agins* and *Penn Central* is based on the proposition that providing a benefit can cure the harm, and that it is all right to let a criminal keep your cash because he will allow you to remain alive. [7]

Current journal articles discuss the legal challenges to short-term rental restrictions. [8] Although a **rational basis is required** to support local ordinances, and although the courts often assume that a rational basis must exist, there is a significant lack of evidence to support current city ordinances that restrict property rental of less than 30 days. [9]

The issue is whether a specific city ordinance **goes to far** and results in overreaching. The court must weigh the evidence to determine if the government action may be classified as overreaching. The meaning of a law may be determined only by a judge. [10]

The facts and circumstances determine whether the ordinance fits one of

---

[7] Douglas W. Kmiec, Inserting the Lost Remaining Pieces Into the Takings Puzzle, 38 *Wm. & Mary L. Rev.* 995, 1018-19 (1997)

[8] Jamila Jefferson-Jones, Airbnb and the Housing Segment of the Modern Sharing Economy: Are Short-Term Rental Restrictions an Unconstitutional Taking, 42 *Hastings Const. L.Q.* 557 (2014-2015). Also see: Roberta A. Kaplan & Michael L. Nadler, Airbnb: A Case Study in Occupancy Regulation and Taxation, 82 *U Chi L Rev Dialogue* 103 (2015). In addition, see: Roberta A. Kaplan , Regulation and the Sharing Economy, *New York Law Journal* (2014).

[9] The rational basis to support city ordinances is typically the unsupported assertion of facts which are contrary to the actual situation. Although fraud upon the Court, this deceptive approach results in suspension of disbelief and acceptance of an absurdity. See: "...in the big lie there is always a certain force of credibility..." https://en.wikiquote.org/wiki/Joseph_Goebbels.

[10] It is emphatically the province and duty of the judicial department to say what the law is....a law repugnant to the constitution is void....the courts ...are bound by that instrument. *Marbury v. Madison*, 5 U.S. 137, 177-179 (1802).

the following classifications:

(1) Mere permissible regulation that is authorized by the police power. For the regulation to be uncompensated, it must have only *de minimus* effects on income or property value.[11]

(2) A draconian regulation which goes to far, as shown by the *significant loss* of future cash flow and resulting property value for the property owner.

This critical classification is solved by measurement, and abiding by the results of measurement. As with many controversial issues involving economics and law, the problem is solved by calculation of the present value of foreseeable loss of future cash for the property owner. The calculation is based on the cash received under two conditions (1) without regulation (2) with regulation. The difference between the two values is the loss of value for the property owner.

Valuation Issues. Significantly, the U.S. Supreme Court has recognized that refined calculation methods allow precise valuation of property rights, based on the present value of future cash flow, even for intangible assets.[12] Dominant federal court decisions hold that loss of marketability results in an additional discount in value based on ownership of a partial interest.[13]

In summary, it is not reasonably questioned that a city ordinance which prevents or unduly restricts short-term rentals results in substantial economic damages, both for the property owners and for the local community. Because of the magnitude of the diminution in value, the result is a violation of substantive due process and requires just compensation for the government taking.

---

[11] William B. Stoebuck, A General Theory of Eminent Domain, 41 *Wash. L. Rev.* 553, 569-71 (1972).

[12] *Newark Morning Ledger v. United States,* 507 U.S. 546 (1993).

[13] For a summary of relevant federal decisions regarding partial interest discounts, see: Farhad Agdhami, Estate Planning for Real Estate Investors (2008*), William & Mary Annual Tax Conference*, paper 47. http://scholarship.law.wm.edu/tax/47.

Discussion of the Santa Monica Ordinance

The Santa Monica Ordinance is shown as an example of the magnitude of economic damages caused by restrictive and draconian city ordinances which pretend to benefit the public, but are actually based on campaign contributions and special interests, such as hotel labor unions and the public interest in low income housing. This type of ordinance is of national importance, because many cities are now proposing similar ordinances.

Economic Damages. The data demonstrates substantial diminution in income and property value resulting from the Santa Monica Ordinance. The detailed calculations on page 45 demonstrate that the foreseeable economic damage over the next decade to Santa Monica property owners caused by the ordinance is $207 million, and the **foreseeable economic damage to local economy is $728 million.**

The economic factors that support the detailed calculation of foreseeable economic damages are shown in *Exhibit A*. The discussion of the method used for calculation of economic damages is shown at page 37. The verbatim wording of the Santa Monica Ordinance is shown by *Exhibit B,* at page 95. This ordinance is a clear violation of California Constitution Article XIIIC, which requires voter approval for a new local tax. The local tax is new because a false classification of a home as a *de facto* hotel does not make a home a hotel. The verbatim wording of the California Senate Bill 593, is shown by *Exhibit C*, at page 107. This Bill proposes government actions which clearly violate Fourth Amendment privacy rights.

The economic magnitude of short-term rentals is substantial. As shown at *Exhibit D*, pages 117-124, for the first seven months of 2015, the gross revenue for Airbnb hosts in the City of Los Angeles was over $65 million, not including gross revenue for HomeAway, Flip Key, and other internet booking agencies.

Although data for cities outside of Los Angeles County are not included in this book, it is clear that it is in the national interest to maintain liberties guaranteed by the U.S. Constitution, and to prevent the substantial economic damage that would be caused by overly restrictive and draconian local laws.

Overview of Recent Court Decisions

In *Pallazo,* the Court recognized that a taking occurs if the government even limits property use. Although property may be regulated to a certain extent, if a regulation goes too far it will be recognized as a taking.

Even if the regulation merely reduces the property value, a taking nonetheless may have occurred, depending on the economic effect on the landowner, the extent of interference with reasonable return on investment, and the character of the government action. The Takings Clause allows a landowner to assert that a particular exercise of the State's regulatory power is so unreasonable or onerous as to compel compensation.

An ordinance which causes future loss of income, such as a new zoning ordinance, is a taking based on the decline in the value of land even without a physical destruction of all of the improvements. An ordinance which is unreasonable does not become less so through passage of time or title. See: *Pennsylvania Coal Co.* v. *Mahon,* 260 U. S. 393 (1922) at 415. Also see: *Penn Central Transp. Co.* v. *New York City,* 438 U. S. 104 (1978), at 124.

Palazzolo v. Rhode Island, 533 U.S. 606 (2001)

....Petitioner filed an inverse condemnation action in Rhode Island Superior Court, asserting that the State's wetlands regulations, as applied by the Council to his parcel, had taken the property without compensation in violation of the Fifth and Fourteenth Amendments. See *id.,* at 45. The suit alleged the Council's action deprived him of "economically, beneficial use" of his property, *ibid.,* resulting in a total taking [616] requiring compensation under *Lucas* v. *South Carolina Coastal Council,* 505 U. S. 1003 (1992). He sought damages in the amount of $3,150,000, a figure derived from an appraiser's estimate as to the value of a 74-lot residential subdivision. The State countered with a host of defenses. After a bench trial, a justice of the Superior Court ruled against petitioner, accepting some of the State's theories. App. to Pet. for Cert. B-1 to B-13.

The Rhode Island Supreme Court affirmed. 746 A. 2d 707 (2000). Like the Superior Court, the State Supreme Court recited multiple grounds for rejecting petitioner's suit. The court held, first, that petitioner's takings claim was not ripe, *id.,* at 712-715; second, that petitioner had no right to challenge regulations predating 1978, when he succeeded to legal ownership of the property from SGI, *id.,* at 716; and third, that the claim of deprivation of all economically beneficial use was contradicted by undisputed evidence that he had $200,000 in development value remaining on an upland parcel of the property, *id.,* at 715. In addition to holding petitioner could not assert a takings claim based on the denial of all economic use, the court concluded he could not recover under the more general test of *Penn Central Transp. Co.* v. *New York City,* 438 U. S. 104 (1978). On this claim, too, the date of acquisition of the parcel was found determinative, and the court held he could have had "no reasonable investment backed expectations that were affected by this regulation" because it predated his ownership, 746 A. 2d, at 717; see also *Penn Central, supra,* at 124.

We disagree with the Supreme Court of Rhode Island as to the first two of these conclusions; and, we hold, the court was correct to conclude that the owner is not deprived of all economic use of his property because the value of upland portions is substantial. We remand for further consideration of the claim under the principles set forth in *Penn Central.*

The Takings Clause of the Fifth Amendment, applicable to the States through the Fourteenth Amendment, *Chicago, B. & Q. R. Co.* v. *Chicago,* 166 U. S. 226 (1897), prohibits the government from taking private property for public use without just compensation. The clearest sort of taking occurs when the government encroaches upon or occupies private land for its own proposed use. Our cases establish that even a minimal "permanent physical occupation of real property" requires compensation under the Clause. *Loretto* v. *Teleprompter Manhattan CATV Corp.,* 458 U. S. 419, 427 (1982). In *Pennsylvania Coal Co.* v. *Mahon,* 260 U. S. 393 (1922), **the Court recognized that there will be instances when government actions do not encroach upon or occupy the property yet still affect and limit its use to such an extent that a taking occurs. In Justice Holmes' well-known, if less than self-defining, formulation, "while property may be regulated to a certain extent, if a regulation goes too far it will be recognized as a taking."** *Id.,* **at 415.**

Since *Mahon,* we have given some, but not too specific, guidance to courts confronted with deciding whether a particular government action goes too far and effects a regulatory taking. First, we have observed, with certain qualifications, see *infra,* at 629-630, that a regulation which "denies all economically beneficial or productive use of land" will require **compensation** under the Takings Clause. *Lucas,* 505 U. S., at 1015; see also *id.,* at 1035 (Kennedy, J., concurring); *Agins* v. *City of Tiburon,* 447 U. S. 255, 261 (1980).

Where a regulation places limitations on land that fall short of eliminating all economically beneficial use, a taking nonetheless may have occurred, depending on a complex of factors including the regulation's economic effect on the landowner, the extent to which the regulation interferes with reasonable investment-backed expectations, and the character of the government action. *Penn Central, supra,* at 124. These inquiries are informed by the purpose of the [618]Takings Clause, which is to prevent the government from "forcing some people alone to bear public burdens which, in all fairness and justice, should be borne by the public as a whole." *Armstrong* v. *United States,* 364 U. S. 40, 49 (1960). ....

The right to improve property, of course, is subject to the reasonable exercise of state authority, including the enforcement of valid zoning and land-use restrictions. See *Pennsylvania Coal Co.,* 260 U. S., at 413 ("Government hardly could go on if to some extent values incident to property could not be diminished without paying for every such change in the general law"). **The Takings Clause, however, in certain circumstances allows a landowner to assert that a particular exercise of the State's regulatory power is so unreasonable or onerous as to compel compensation. Just as a prospective enactment, such as a new zoning ordinance, can limit the value of land without effecting a taking because it can be understood as reasonable by all concerned, other enactments are unreasonable and do not become less so through passage of time or title.**

Were we to accept the State's rule, the postenactment transfer of title would absolve the State of its obligation to defend any action restricting land use, no matter how extreme or unreasonable. A State would be allowed, in effect, to put an expiration date on the Takings Clause. This ought not to be the rule. Future generations, too, have a right to challenge unreasonable limitations on the use and value of land.

Nor does the justification of notice take into account the effect on owners at the time of enactment, who are prejudiced as well. Should an owner attempt to challenge a new regulation, but not survive the process of ripening his or her claim (which, as this case demonstrates, will often take years), under the proposed rule the right to **compensation** may not be asserted by an heir or successor, and so may not be asserted at all. The State's rule would work a critical alteration to the nature of property, as the newly regulated landowner is stripped of the ability to transfer the interest which was possessed prior to the regulation.

The State may not by this means secure a windfall for itself. See *Webb's Fabulous Pharmacies, Inc.* v. *Beckwith,* 449 U. S. [628] 155, 164 (1980) ("[A] State, by *ipse dixit,* may not transform private property into public property without **compensation**"); cf. Ellickson, Property in

Land, 102 Yale L. J. 1315, 1368-1369 (1993) (right to transfer interest in land is a defining characteristic of the fee simple estate). The proposed rule is, furthermore, capricious in effect. The young owner contrasted with the older owner, the owner with the resources to hold contrasted with the owner with the need to sell, would be in different positions. The Takings Clause is not so quixotic. A blanket rule that purchasers with notice have no compensation right when a claim becomes ripe is **too blunt an instrument to accord with the duty to compensate for what is taken.**

Direct condemnation, by invocation of the State's power of eminent domain, presents different considerations from cases alleging a taking based on a burdensome regulation. In a direct condemnation action, or when a State has physically invaded the property without filing suit, the fact and extent of the taking are known. In such an instance, it is a general rule of the law of eminent domain that any award goes to the owner at the time of the taking, and that the right to compensation is not passed to a subsequent purchaser. See *Danforth* v. *United States,* 308 U. S. 271, 284 (1939); 2 Sackman, Eminent Domain, at § 5.01[5][d][i] ("It is well settled that when there is a taking of property by eminent domain in compliance with the law, it is the owner of the property *at the time of the taking* who is entitled to compensation").

A challenge to the application of a land-use regulation, by contrast, does not mature until ripeness requirements have been satisfied, under principles we have discussed; until this point an inverse condemnation claim alleging a regulatory taking cannot be maintained. It would be illogical, and unfair, to bar a regulatory takings claim because of the postenactment transfer of ownership where the steps necessary to make the claim ripe were not taken, or could not have been taken, by a previous owner. [629]

There is controlling precedent for our conclusion. *Nollan* v. *California Coastal Comm'n,* 483 U. S. 825 (1987), presented the question whether it was consistent with the Takings Clause for a state regulatory agency to require oceanfront landowners to provide lateral beach access to the public as the condition for a development permit. The principal dissenting opinion observed it was a policy of the California Coastal Commission to require the condition, and that the Nollans, who purchased their home after the policy went into effect, were "on notice that new developments would be approved only if provisions were made for lateral beach access." *Id.,* at 860 (Brennan, J., dissenting). A majority of the Court rejected the proposition. "So long as the Commission could not have deprived the prior owners of the easement without compensating them," the Court reasoned, "the prior owners must be understood to have transferred their full property rights in conveying the lot." *Id.,* at 834, n. 2.

11

It is argued that *Nollan*'s holding was limited by the later decision in *Lucas* v. *South Carolina Coastal Council,* 505 U. S. 1003 (1992). In *Lucas* the Court observed that a landowner's ability to recover for a government deprivation of all economically beneficial use of property is not absolute but instead is confined by limitations on the use of land which "inhere in the title itself." *Id.,* at 1029. This is so, the Court reasoned, because the landowner is constrained by those "restrictions that background principles of the State's law of property and nuisance already place upon land ownership." *Ibid.*

It is asserted here that *Lucas* stands for the proposition that any new regulation, once enacted, becomes a background principle of property law which cannot be challenged by those who acquire title after the enactment. We have no occasion to consider the precise circumstances when a legislative enactment can be deemed a background principle of state law or whether those circumstances are present here. **It suffices to say that a regulation that otherwise [630] would be unconstitutional absent compensation is not transformed into a background principle of the State's law by mere virtue of the passage of title.** This relative standard would be incompatible with our description of the concept in *Lucas,* which is explained in terms of those common, shared understandings of permissible limitations derived from a State's legal tradition, see *id.,* at 1029-1030.

A regulation or common-law rule cannot be a background principle for some owners but not for others. The determination whether an existing, general law can limit all economic use of property must turn on objective factors, such as the nature of the land use proscribed. See *id.,* at 1030 ("The `total taking' inquiry we require today will ordinarily entail . . . analysis of, among other things, the degree of harm to public lands and resources, or adjacent private property, posed by the claimant's proposed activities"). A law does not become a background principle for subsequent owners by enactment itself. *Lucas* did not overrule our holding in *Nollan,* which, as we have noted, is based on essential Takings Clause principles. ***Palazzolo v. Rhode Island,* 533 U.S. 606 (2001)**

12

In *Goldblatt,* the U.S. Supreme Court noted that the Fifth Amendment **requires compensation for property taken for public use**. However, if the government proves that the prohibition is necessary due *to risk of injury to health, morals, or safety* of the community, or proves *noxious use* of the property, then the taking does not require compensation.

For short term rental circumstances, with prior screening of the guest background and reviews from prior hosts, there is NO reasonable risk of injury to health, morals, or safety. Accordingly, due to lack of noxious use, there is NO valid exercise of police power for short term rental circumstances.

Goldblatt v. Hempstead, 369 U.S. 590 (1962)

...Concededly the ordinance completely prohibits a beneficial use to which the property has previously been devoted. However, such a characterization does not tell us whether or not the ordinance is unconstitutional. It is an oft-repeated truism that every regulation necessarily speaks as a prohibition. If this ordinance is otherwise a valid exercise of the town's police powers, the fact that it deprives the property of its most beneficial use does not render it unconstitutional. *Walls* v. *Midland Carbon Co.,* 254 U. S. 300 (1920); *Hadacheck* v. *Sebastian,* 239 U. S. [593] 394 (1915); *Reinman* v. *Little Rock,* 237 U. S. 171 (1915); *Mugler v. Kansas,* 123 U. S. 623 (1887); see *Laurel Hill Cemetery* v. *San Francisco,* 216 U. S. 358 (1910).

As pointed out in *Mugler v. Kansas, supra,* at 668-669: "[T]he present case must be governed by principles that do not involve the power of **eminent domain, in the exercise of which property may not be taken for public use without compensation. A prohibition simply upon the use of property for purposes that are declared, by valid legislation, to be injurious to the health, morals, or safety of the community, cannot, in any just sense, be deemed a taking or an appropriation of property for the public benefit.**

Such legislation does not disturb the owner in the control or use of his property for lawful purposes, nor restrict his right to dispose of it, but is only a declaration by the State that its use by any one, for certain forbidden purposes, is prejudicial to the public interests. . . . **The power which the States have of prohibiting such use by individuals of their property as will be prejudicial to the health, the morals, or the safety of the public,** is not—and, consistently with the existence and safety of organized society, cannot be—burdened with the condition that the State

13

must compensate such individual owners for pecuniary losses they may sustain, by reason of their **not being permitted, by a noxious use of their property, to inflict injury upon the community.**" Nor is it of controlling significance that the "use" prohibited here is of the soil itself as opposed to a "use" upon the soil, cf. *United States* v. *Central Eureka Mining Co., 357 U. S. 155 (1958),* or that the use prohibited is arguably not a common-law nuisance, *e. g., Reinman* v. *Little Rock, supra.* [594]

This is not to say, however, that governmental action in the form of regulation cannot be so onerous as to constitute a taking which constitutionally requires compensation. *Pennsylvania Coal Co.* v. *Mahon, 260 U. S. 393 (1922)*; see *United States* v. *Central Eureka Mining Co., supra.* **There is no set formula to determine where regulation ends and taking begins. Although a comparison of values before and after is relevant**, see *Pennsylvania Coal Co.* v. *Mahon, supra,* it is by no means conclusive, see *Hadacheck* v. *Sebastian, supra,* where a diminution in value from $800,000 to $60,000 was upheld.

How far regulation may go before it becomes a taking we need not now decide, for **there is no evidence in the present record** which even remotely suggests that prohibition of further mining will reduce the value of the lot in question.[3] Indulging in the usual presumption of constitutionality, *infra,* p. 596, we find no indication that the prohibitory effect of Ordinance No. 16 is sufficient to render it an unconstitutional taking if it is otherwise a valid police regulation.

The question, therefore, narrows to whether the prohibition of further excavation below the water table is a valid exercise of the town's police power. The term "police power" connotes the time-tested conceptional limit of public encroachment upon private interests. Except for the substitution of the familiar standard of "reasonableness," **this Court has generally refrained from announcing any specific criteria.** The classic statement of the rule in *Lawton* v. *Steele, 152 U. S. 133, 137 (1894),* is still valid today:

"To justify the State in . . . interposing its authority in behalf of the public, it must appear, first, that [595] the interests of the public . . . require such interference; and, second, that the means are reasonably necessary for the accomplishment of the purpose, and not unduly oppressive upon individuals."

Even this rule is not applied with strict precision, for this Court has often said that "debatable questions as to reasonableness are not for the courts but for the legislature . . . ." *E. g., Sproles* v. *Binford, 286 U. S. 374, 388 (1932).* The ordinance in question was **passed as a safety measure**, and the town is attempting to uphold it on that basis. To evaluate its reasonableness we therefore need to know such things as **the nature of the menace against which it will protect, the availability**

and effectiveness of other less drastic protective steps, and the loss which appellants will suffer from the imposition of the ordinance......

Although one could imagine that preventing further deepening of a pond already 25 feet deep would have a *de minimis* effect on public safety, we cannot say that such a conclusion is compelled by facts of which we can take notice. Even if we could draw such a conclusion, [596] we would be unable to say the ordinance is unreasonable; for all we know, the ordinance may have a *de minimis* effect on appellants.

Our past cases leave no doubt that appellants had the burden on "reasonableness." *E. g., Bibb* v. *Navajo Freight Lines,* 359 U. S. 520, 529 (1959) (exercise of police power is presumed to be constitutionally valid); *Salsburg* v. *Maryland,* 346 U. S. 545, 553 (1954) (the presumption of reasonableness is with the State); *United States* v. *Carolene Products Co.,* 304 U. S. 144, 154 (1938) (exercise of police power will be upheld if any state of facts either known or which could be reasonably assumed affords support for it).

This burden not having been met, the prohibition of excavation on the 20-acre-lake tract must stand as a valid police regulation. *Goldblatt v. Hempstead,* 369 U.S. 590 (1962)

The Fifth Amendment protects private property by providing that any government action that decreases the value of the property or decreases the foreseeable income from use of the property requires just compensation for the taking. Although this absolute protection is argued to be qualified by the police power of a city, human nature will extend the absolute protection more and more until at last private property disappears. Such city intrusion on property rights is prohibited by the Fifth Amendment. Generally, although property rights may be regulated to a certain extent, **if regulation goes too far it will be recognized as a taking.** Even a strong public desire to improve the public condition still requires the government to pay for the change.

Pennsylvania Coal Co. v. Mahon, 260 U.S. 393 (1922)

The protection of private property in the Fifth Amendment presupposes that it is wanted for public use, but provides that **it shall not be taken for such use without compensation**. A similar assumption is made in the decisions upon the Fourteenth **Amendment**. *Hairston* v. *Danville & Western Ry. Co.,* 208 U.S. 598, 605. When this seemingly absolute protection is found to be qualified by the police power, **the natural tendency of human nature is to extend the qualification more and more until at last private property disappears. But that cannot be accomplished in this way under the Constitution of the United States.**

The general rule at least is, that while property may be regulated to a certain extent, if regulation goes too far it will be recognized as a taking. It may be doubted how far exceptional cases, like the blowing up of a house to stop a conflagration, go — and if they go beyond the general rule, [416] whether they do not stand as much upon tradition as upon principle. *Bowditch* v. *Boston,* 101 U.S. 16. In general it is **not** plain that a man's misfortunes or necessities will justify his shifting the damages to his neighbor's shoulders. *Spade* v. *Lynn & Boston R.R. Co.,* 172 Mass. 488, 489. **We are in danger of forgetting that a strong public desire to improve the public condition is not enough to warrant achieving the desire by a shorter cut than the constitutional way of paying for the change.** As we already have said, this is a question of degree — and therefore cannot be disposed of by general propositions. *Pennsylvania Coal Co. v. Mahon,* 260 U.S. 393 (1922)

As explained in Coniston, property is a bundle of rights, and if the state confers rights with one hand and takes them away with the other by a zoning decision that deprives the owner of a property right, then the property owner is denied substantive due process, even without considering the Fifth Amendment just compensation.

In the context of judicial review, an ordinance that is not "shown to have any `substantial relation to the public health, safety, morals or general welfare'" and that "cuts deeply into a fundamental right associated with the ownership of residential property" violates the Constitution. See: *Moore v. City of East Cleveland, supra,* 431 U.S. at 520, 97 S.Ct. at 1946.

Coniston Corp. v. Village of Hoffman Estates, 844 F.2d 461 (7th Cir 1988).

The taking is complete when it occurs, and the duty to pay just compensation arises then, see, e.g., *First Evangelical Lutheran Church v. County of Los Angeles, ___ U.S. ___,* 107 S.Ct. 2378, 2389 n. 10, 96 L.Ed.2d 250 (1987), **but the suit for just compensation is not ripe until it is apparent that the state does not intend to pay compensation,** *Williamson County Regional Planning Comm'n v. Hamilton Bank,* 473 U.S. 172, 194, 105 S.Ct. 3108, 3121, 87 L.Ed.2d 126 (1985); *Unity Ventures v. County of Lake,* 841 F.2d 770, 773-74 (7th Cir.1988). These plaintiffs have not explored the possibility of obtaining compensation for an alleged regulatory taking. In fact, they do [464] not want compensation; they want their site plan approved.

One might have thought that the takings clause would occupy the field of constitutional remedies for governmental actions that deprive people of their property, and hence that the plaintiffs' waiver of their takings claim would drag their due process claims down with it. But this is not correct; pushed to its logical extreme, the argument would read "property" out of the due process clause of the Fifth and Fourteenth Amendments. Even limited to claims of denial of substantive due process the argument may fail.

Rather than being viewed simply as a limitation on governmental power **the takings clause could be viewed as the source of a governmental privilege: to take property for public use upon payment of the market value of that property, since "just compensation" has been held to be satisfied by payment of market value,** see, e.g., *United States v. Reynolds,* 397 U.S. 14, 16, 90 S.Ct. 803, 805, 25 L.Ed.2d 12 (1970).

Compensation in the constitutional sense is therefore not full compensation, for market value is not the value that every owner of property attaches to his property but merely the value that the marginal owner attaches to *his* property. Many owners are "intramarginal," meaning that because of relocation costs, sentimental attachments, or the special suitability of the property for their particular (perhaps idiosyncratic) needs, they value their property at more than its market value (i.e., it is not "for sale"). Such owners are hurt when the government takes their property and gives them just its market value in return. The taking in effect confiscates the additional (call it "personal") value that they obtain from the property, but this limited confiscation is permitted provided the taking is for a public use.

It can be argued that if the taking is not for a public use, it is unconstitutional, but perhaps not as a taking; for all the takings clause says is "nor shall private property be taken for public use, without just compensation." This language specifies a consequence if property is taken for a public use but is silent on the consequences if property is taken for a private one. Perhaps the effect of this silence is to dump the case into the due process clause. The taking would then be a deprivation of property without due process of law. The victim could bring suit under section 1983 against the governmental officials who took or are threatening to take his property, seeking an injunction against the taking (or an order to return the property if, it has been taken already — subject to whatever defense the Eleventh Amendment might afford against such a remedy) or full tort damages, not just market value.

There are two objections to this approach. First, the takings clause may be broad enough to take care of the problem without the help of the due process clause. The Supreme Court may believe that **the takings clause, of its own force, forbids any governmental taking not for a public use, even if just compensation is tendered**.... see, e.g., *Hawaii Housing Authority v. Midkiff,* 467 U.S. 229, 241, 104 S.Ct. 2321, 2329, 81 L.Ed.2d 186 (1984), though it may be inadvertent, and there is language in some cases that looks the other way ...compare *First English Evangelical Lutheran Church v. County of Los Angeles,* ___ U.S. ___, 107 S.Ct. 2378, 2385, 96 L.Ed.2d 250 (1987), with *id.* 107 S.Ct. at 2386 (takings clause requires compensation "in the event of otherwise proper interference amounting to a taking").

18

In *Midkiff* the Court cited, as an example of a case where it had "invalidated a compensated taking of property for lack of a justifying public purpose," 467 U.S. at 241, 104 S.Ct. at 2329, a case (*Missouri Pac. Ry. v. Nebraska,* 164 U.S. 403, 417, 17 S.Ct. 130, 135, 41 L.Ed. 489 (1896)) where in fact the Court, after finding there was no public use, had held that the state had denied the owner due process of law. In other words, once the privilege created by the takings clause was stripped away, the state was exposed as having taken a person's property without due process of law. But this was before the takings clause had been held applicable to the states (via the due process clause of the Fourteenth Amendment) in *Chicago, Burlington &* [465] *Quincy R.R. v. City of Chicago,* 166 U.S. 226, 236, 17 S.Ct. 581, 584, 41 L.Ed. 979 (1897) — though only a year before.

It seems odd that the takings clause would require just compensation when property was taken for a public use yet grant no remedy when the property was taken for a private use, although the semantics of the clause are consistent with such an interpretation, as we have seen. Yet well after the takings clause was deemed absorbed into the due process clause of the Fourteenth **Amendment**, the Supreme Court reviewed a zoning ordinance for conformity to substantive due process. See *Euclid v. Ambler Realty Co.,* 272 U.S. 365, 47 S.Ct. 114, 71 L.Ed. 303 (1926).

Justice Stevens has said that the Court in *Euclid* "fused the two express constitutional restrictions on any state interference with private property — that property shall not be taken without due process nor for a public purpose without just compensation — into a single standard." *Moore v. City of East Cleveland,* 431 U.S. 494, 514, 97 S.Ct. 1932, 1943, 52 L.Ed.2d 531 (1977) (concurring opinion).

The other objection to the due process route in a case such as the present one is that it depends on the idea of "substantive" due process. This is the idea that depriving a person of life, liberty, or property can violate the due process clause of the Fifth and Fourteenth Amendments even if there are no procedural irregularities — even if, for example, the state after due deliberation has passed a statute establishing procedures for taking private homes and giving them to major campaign contributors or people with red hair, and in taking the plaintiff's home has complied scrupulously with the statute's procedural requirements.

Substantive due process is a tenacious but embattled concept. Text and history, at least ancient history, are against it, though perhaps not decisively. (See generally Jurow, *Untimely Thoughts: A Reconsideration of the Origins of Due Process of Law,* 19 Am.J. Legal Hist. 265 (1975).)

A provision which states that life, liberty, or property may not be taken without due process of law implies that life, liberty, or property *can* be taken with due process of law, and hence that the only limitations are procedural ones.

The term "due process of law" has been traced back to a fourteenth-century English statute, in which the term plainly referred to procedure rather than substance. See 28 Edw. III, ch. 3 (1354) ("no man ... shall be put out of land ..., nor taken, nor imprisoned, nor disinherited, nor put to death, without being brought into answer by due process of law"). In the seventeenth century Sir Edward Coke confused the picture by equating the term to Magna Carta's much vaguer expression "by the law of the land." The Supreme Court adopted Coke's approach in *Murray's Lessee v. Hoboken Land & Improvement Co.,* 59 U.S. (18 How.) 272, 276, 15 L.Ed. 372 (1856), pointing out that the Northwest Ordinance and several state constitutions had used the Magna Carta language and implying that the terminology was interchangeable in the Fifth Amendment as well. ...

It also and by the same token invites the federal courts to sit in judgment on almost all state action — including, to come back to the present case, all zoning decisions. For it is tempting to view every zoning decision that is adverse to the landowner and in violation of state law as a deprivation of property.

Property is not a thing, but a bundle of rights, and if the state confers rights with one hand and takes them away with the other, by a zoning decision that by violating [466] state law deprives the owner of a property right and not just a property interest (the owner's financial interest in being able to employ his land in its most valuable use), why is it not guilty of denying substantive due process?

No one thinks substantive due process should be interpreted so broadly as to protect landowners against erroneous zoning decisions. But it is difficult to come up with limiting concepts that are not completely ad hoc. Justice Stevens tried — though in the context of judicial review of an ordinance, rather than of an individual decision applying an ordinance — in his concurring opinion in *Moore v. City of East Cleveland, supra,* 431 U.S. at 520, 97 S.Ct. at 1946, where he suggested that **an ordinance that is not "shown to have any `substantial relation to the public health, safety, morals or general welfare'" and that "cuts deeply into a fundamental right associated with the ownership of residential property" violates the Constitution.**

The present case is so remote from a plausible violation of substantive due process that we need not decide whether, or to precisely what extent, the concept limits takings by state and local governments; .... or, finally, whether the plaintiffs can force us to confront difficult questions of substantive due process by their decision to waive a seemingly more straightforward claim under the takings clause.

The Village of Hoffman Estates did not *take* the plaintiffs' land (or in the language of the due process clause, deprive them of the land) for a *private* (hence presumptively unreasonable) purpose, so even if we assume that if both conditions were fulfilled the taking or deprivation would violate the due process clause, the plaintiffs cannot prevail.

As to whether there was a deprivation: Granted, the rejection of the plaintiffs' site plan probably reduced the value of their land. The plan must have represented their best guess about how to maximize the value of the property, and almost certainly a better guess than governmental officials would make even if the officials were trying to maximize that value, which of course they were not. But the plaintiffs **do not even argue that the rejection of the site plan reduced the value of their parcel much**, let alone that the parcel will be worthless unless it can be used to create 181,000 square feet of office space.

A taking is actionable under the takings clause even if it is of just a sliver of the owner's property (e.g., a one-foot strip at the back of a 100-acre estate), see *Loretto v. Teleprompter Manhattan CATV Corp., 458 U.S. 419, 102 S.Ct. 3164, 73 L.Ed.2d 868 (1982),* and we can assume that the same thing is true under the due process clause. But in cases under the takings clause the courts distinguish between **taking away all of the owner's rights to a small part** of his land and **taking away (through regulation) a few of his rights to all of his land,** and grant much broader protection in the first case. With *Loretto* compare *City of Eastlake v. Forest City Enterprises, Inc., 426 U.S. 668,* 674 and n. 8, 96 S.Ct. 2358, 2362 and n. 8, 49 L.Ed.2d 132 (1976); *Barbian v. Panagis, 694 F.2d 476, 483-85 (7th Cir.1982),* and cases cited there.

The plaintiffs in this case have been deprived of their "right" to create 181,000 square feet of office space on a 17-acre parcel of a much larger tract, and that deprivation is a limited, perhaps minimal, incursion into their property rights. If so it is not a deprivation at all, in the constitutional sense, and the due process clause is not in play. See *Wells Fargo Armored Service Corp. v. Georgia Public Service Comm'n, 547 F.2d 938, 941 (5th Cir.1977);* cf. *Brown v. Brienen, 722 F.2d 360, 364 (7th Cir.1983)* (dictum); *York v. City of Cedartown, 648 F.2d 231 (5th Cir.1981)* (per curiam). ***Coniston Corp. v. Village of Hoffman Estates*, 844 F.2d 461 (7th Cir 1988)**

Although some judges might view *Carmel* as a precedent, the *Carmel* decision merely reflects an incorrect decision which was not appealed to the U.S. Supreme Court. In *Carmel,* the Court of Appeals 6th District held that a local ordinance prohibiting short term rentals in a R-1 zone was not void under procedural due process grounds. The following issues distinguish *Carmel,* so *res judicata* or collateral estoppel are not applicable to the Santa Monica case.

1. In *Carmel*, the court comments regarding Fifth Amendment taking were merely dicta, because the court remarks were not necessary for the decision, *Redevelopment Agency v. Gilmore*, 38 Cal.3d 790, 799. Judicial estoppel cannot apply when the party against whom the earlier decision is asserted did not have a "full and fair opportunity" to litigate that issue in the earlier case. *Montana v. United States* (1979) 440 U.S. 147 at 153; *Blonder-Tongue Laboratories v. University of Illinois Foundation* (1971) 401 U.S. 313, 328-329. Although the court discussed Fifth Amendment taking, the Plaintiffs failed to present evidence or arguments to support their potential Fifth Amendment claims. There is "... a sound judicial policy against applying collateral estoppel in cases which concern matters of important public interest...", *Chern v. Bank of America* (1976) 15 Cal.3d 866, 872.

2. The *Carmel* circumstances are not sufficiently similar to the Santa Monica circumstances. *Carmel* concerned only R-1 zoning restrictions, but Santa Monica has conceded specific types of short term rentals in R-1 zone.

3. *Carmel* is a 6th District decision which is not binding on Santa Monica, which is in the 2nd District. There is NO California Supreme Court decision and NO U.S. Supreme Court decision on the *Carmel* issues.

4. Zoning regulations are founded in the state police power, which is justified only if this power clearly supports the public welfare. Police power is limited by the specific facts and circumstances, *Euclid v. Ambler Co., supra,* 272 U.S. at p. 387. A void city ordinance is demonstrated by *de minimus* public welfare benefit compared to substantial economic damages for property owners.

5. When a city ordinance conflicts with a Constitutional right, the ordinance is deemed facially invalid and unconstitutional, *Los Angeles v. Patel*, 135 S.Ct. 2443 (2015), decided on Forth Amendment grounds.

Ewing v. City of Carmel-By-The-Sea,
34 Cal.App.3d 1579 (6th Cir 1991)

Plaintiff homeowners challenge the constitutionality of a zoning ordinance prohibiting transient commercial use of residential property for remuneration for less than 30 consecutive days. The trial court upheld the ordinance. We affirm.

Plaintiffs are owners of single-family, residential property zoned R-1 in the City of Carmel-by-the-Sea. Plaintiffs challenge Ordinance No. 89-17...May 1989...The ordinance prohibits the "Transient Commercial Use of Residential Property for Remuneration ... in the R-1 District."

The ordinance defines the "transient commercial use of residential property" as "the commercial use, by any person, of Residential Property for bed and breakfast, hostel, hotel, inn, lodging, motel, resort or other transient lodging uses where the term of occupancy, possession or tenancy of the property by the person entitled to such occupancy, possession or tenancy is for less than thirty (30) consecutive calendar days." ...In August 1989, the trial court preliminarily enjoined Carmel from enforcement of the ordinance.... The trial court permanently enjoined enforcement of the 1981 ordinance, finding it to be "unconstitutional as it invades the rights of association, privacy, and due process. The Court further finds that the Ordinance is over-broad and does not substantially effect its stated goals." Carmel did not appeal. ...

(2a) We turn to the constitutionality of Ordinance No. 89-17, beginning with plaintiffs' argument that the ordinance constitutes a "taking" in violation of the Fifth Amendment. (U.S. Const., 5th Amend. ["No person shall be ... deprived of ... property, without due process of law; nor shall private property be taken for public use, without just compensation."]; *Chicago, Burlington &c. R'd* v. *Chicago* (1897) 166 U.S. 226, 235-241 [41 L.Ed. 979, 984-986, 17 S.Ct. 581] [Fifth Amendment applies to the states through the Fourteenth Amendment].) **Although plaintiffs offer their "taking" argument almost as an afterthought by way of supplemental briefing,** we view it as the logical starting point for our constitutional analysis.

The dawn of the 20th century marked the beginning of zoning laws in this country. (*Euclid* v. *Ambler Co.* (1926) 272 U.S. 365, 386 [71 L.Ed. 303, 310, 47 S.Ct. 114, 54 A.L.R. 1016].) Until then, "urban life was comparatively simple...." (*Ibid.*) But the "great increase and concentration of population" and "the advent of automobiles and rapid transit street railways" [1587] created problems necessitating land-use regulation. (*Id.* at pp. 386-387 [71 L.Ed. at p. 310].) ...The Supreme

Court declared that zoning regulations must find their justification in the police power, asserted for the public welfare. (*Euclid* v. *Ambler Co., supra,* 272 U.S. at p. 387 [71 L.Ed. at p. 310].) The court noted that **the extent of the police power "varies with circumstances and conditions."** (*Ibid.*) Likewise, "while the meaning of constitutional guaranties never varies, **the scope of their application must expand or contract to meet the new and different conditions which are constantly coming within the field of their operation."** (*Ibid.*)...

The Supreme Court upheld the Euclid ordinances as a proper exercise of the police power. The court concluded that even if Euclid's reasons for adopting the scheme, such as the preservation of residential areas, "do not demonstrate the wisdom or sound policy in all respects of those restrictions which we have indicated as pertinent to the inquiry, at least, the reasons are sufficiently cogent to preclude us from saying, as it must be said before the ordinance can be declared unconstitutional, that such provisions are clearly arbitrary and unreasonable, having no substantial relation to the public health, safety, morals, or general welfare." (*Euclid* v. *Ambler Co., supra,* 272 U.S. at p. 395 [71 L.Ed. at p. 314].) [1588] ....

Like the court in *Euclid,* the court in *Miller* stressed the elasticity of the police power: "as a commonwealth develops politically, economically, and socially, the police power likewise develops, **within reason,** to meet the changed and changing conditions. What was at one time regarded as an improper exercise of the police power may now, because of changed living conditions, be recognized as a legitimate exercise of that power." (*Miller* v. *Board of Public Works, supra,* 195 Cal. at p. 484; see current Cal. Const., art. XI, § 7 [a city may "make and enforce within its limits all local, police, sanitary, and other ordinances and regulations **not in conflict with general laws**"].) ....

The law has also evolved, but the basic principles survive. (3) Zoning ordinances are still presumptively constitutional. (*Goldblatt* v. *Hempstead* (1962) 369 U.S. 590, 594 [8 L.Ed.2d 130, 133-134, 82 S.Ct. 987]; *Associated Home Builders etc., Inc.* v. *City of Livermore* (1976) 18 Cal.3d 582, 604-605 [135 Cal. Rptr. 41, 557 P.2d 473, 92 A.L.R.3d 1038].) But "[t]he application of a general zoning law to particular property **effects a taking if** [1589] the ordinance **does not substantially advance legitimate state interests**, see *Nectow* v. *Cambridge,* 277 U.S. 183, 188 (1928), or **denies an owner economically viable use of his land**, see *Penn Central Transp. Co.* v. *New York City,* 438 U.S. 104, 138, n. 36 (1978). The determination **that governmental action constitutes a taking is, in essence, a determination that the public at large, rather than a single owner, must bear the burden of an exercise of state power in the public interest.** Although no precise rule determines when property has been taken, see *Kaiser Aetna* v. *United States,* 444 U.S. 164

24

(1979), **the question necessarily requires a weighing of private and public interests."** (*Agins* v. *Tiburon* (1980) 447 U.S. 255, 260-261 [65 L.Ed.2d 106, 112, 100 S.Ct. 2138].)

.... The council found that the use of single-family residential property for transient lodging was a commercial use inconsistent with the purpose of the R-1 District. .... **Plaintiffs submit declarations intended to show that transient use of R-1 property does not create the "unmitigatable, adverse impacts" cited by the council. ...** [1590] **District. She found no complaints regarding "light and glare," "noise," or "transient rental use."** ....In *Miller* and *Euclid,* the highest courts of this state and of the land recognized that maintenance of the character of residential neighborhoods is a proper purpose of zoning. The California Supreme Court employed language now a bit dated yet plainly relevant to the case at hand: "[W]e think it may be safely and sensibly said that justification for residential zoning may, in the last analysis, be rested upon the protection of the civic and social values of the American home. ...." (*Miller* v. *Board of Public Works, supra,* 195 Cal. at p. 493.) ...[159] **It stands to reason that the "residential character" of a neighborhood is threatened when a significant number of homes — at least 12 percent in this case, according to the record — are occupied not by permanent residents but by a stream of tenants staying a weekend, a week, or even 29 days. ...**

Plaintiffs attempt to equate this case with *Parr* v. *Municipal Court* (1971) 3 Cal.3d 861 [92 Cal. Rptr. 153, 479 P.2d 353], in which the Supreme Court confronted a Carmel zoning ordinance prohibiting, among other things, sitting or lying upon a public lawn. .... The court concluded that the ordinance **violated appellant's right of equal protection by discriminating against a social class**. Plaintiffs quote from the concurrence in *Building Industry Assn.* v. *City of Camarillo* (1986) 41 Cal.3d 810, 825 [226 Cal. Rptr. 81, 718 P.2d 68]: "An impermissible elitist concept is invoked when a community constructs a legal moat around its perimeter to exclude all or most outsiders." Plaintiffs argue that the ordinance challenged in *Parr* and Ordinance No. 89-17 demonstrate Carmel's desire to build a legal moat. The ordinance challenged in *Parr* was struck down; thus, plaintiffs reason, Ordinance No. 89-17 should meet the same fate.

.... (5) A zoning ordinance does not constitute a taking simply because it narrows a property owner's options. In fact, "[m]any zoning ordinances place limits on the property owner's right to make profitable use of some segments of his property." (*Keystone Bituminous Coal Assn.* v. *DeBenedictis* (1987) 480 U.S. 470, 498 [94 L.Ed.2d 472, 496, 107 S.Ct. 1232]; see, e.g., *Griffin Development Co.* v. *City of Oxnard* (1985) 39 Cal.3d 256 [217 Cal. Rptr. 1, 703 P.2d 339] [condominium conversion ordinance]; *Birkenfeld* v. *City of Berkeley* (1976) 17 Cal.3d

25

129 [130 Cal. Rptr. 465, 550 P.2d 1001] [rent control law].) Justice Holmes stated the test in *Penna. Coal Co.* v. *Mahon* (1922) 260 U.S. 393, 413 [67 L.Ed. 322, 325, 43 S.Ct. 158, 28 A.L.R. 1321]: "Government hardly could go on if to some extent values incident to property could not be diminished without paying for every such change in the general law. As long recognized, some values are enjoyed under an implied limitation and must yield to the police power. **But obviously the implied limitation must have its limits, or the contract and due process clauses are gone.** One fact for consideration in determining such limits is **the extent of the diminution. When it reaches a certain magnitude, in most if not in all cases there must be an exercise of eminent domain and compensation to sustain the act**. So the question depends upon the particular facts." ....

Plaintiffs also complain that Carmel has drawn the line arbitrarily by permitting rentals of 30 consecutive days but not 29. Line drawing is the essence of zoning.... In *Euclid,* the Supreme Court recognized that "**in some fields, the bad fades into the good by such insensible degrees that the two are not capable of being readily distinguished and separated in terms of legislation.**" (*Euclid* v. *Ambler Co., supra,* 272 U.S. at p. 389 [71 L.Ed. at p. 311].) Nonetheless, the line must be drawn, and the legislature must do it. Absent an arbitrary or unreasonable delineation, **it is not the prerogative of the courts to second-guess the legislative decision.** (See *Village of Belle Terre* v. *Boraas* (1974) 416 U.S. 1, 8 [39 L.Ed.2d 797, 803-804, 94 S.Ct. 1536]; *Berman* v. *Parker* (1954) 348 U.S. 26, 35-36 [99 L.Ed. 27, 39-40, 75 S.Ct. 98].)

In this case, it appears that Carmel did not wish to discourage month-to-month tenancies. Indeed, long-term tenants may create as stable a community as resident homeowners. Through Ordinance No. 89-17, Carmel wished to curtail only short-term occupancies for remuneration. **We believe that the 30-day cutoff is not arbitrary but, rather, is reasonably linked to that goal. (See Rev. & Tax. Code, § 7280 [establishing 30-day cutoff for city or county tax upon short-term occupancy in "hotel, inn, tourist home or house, motel, or other lodging"]; Civ. Code, § 1943 [tenancy presumed to be month-to-month unless otherwise designated in writing].)**

(7a) Plaintiffs offer yet another Fifth Amendment argument, contending that Ordinance No. 89-17 is unconstitutionally vague and overbroad. [1594] (8) Indeed, "a **statute which either forbids or requires the doing of an act in terms so vague that men of common intelligence must necessarily guess at its meaning and differ as to its application, violates the first essential of due process.**" (*Connally* v. *General Const. Co.* (1926) 269 U.S. 385, 391 [70 L.Ed. 322, 328, 46 S.Ct. 126].) In *Grayned* v. *City of Rockford* (1972) 408 U.S. 104, 108 [33

L.Ed.2d 222, 227, 92 S.Ct. 2294], the Supreme Court observed that a vague law may offend "several important values." First, the person of ordinary intelligence should have a **reasonable opportunity to know what is prohibited**. A vague law may trap the innocent by **not providing fair warning**. Second, a vague law **impermissibly delegates the legislative job** of defining what is prohibited to policemen, judges, and juries, creating a danger of arbitrary and discriminatory application. Third, a **vague law may have a chilling effect**, causing people to steer a wider course than necessary in order to avoid the strictures of the law.

Yet, "[c]ondemned to the use of words, we can never expect mathematical certainty from our language." (*Grayned* v. *City of Rockford, supra,* 408 U.S. at p. 110 [33 L.Ed.2d at pp. 228-229], fn. omitted.) (9) "Often the requisite standards of certainty can be fleshed out from otherwise vague statutory language by reference to any of the following sources: (1) long established or commonly accepted usage; (2) usage at common law; (3) judicial interpretations of the statutory language or of similar language; (4) legislative history or purpose. [Citation.] While **the dangers of discriminatory enforcement and ex post facto punishment posed by vague penal provisions must be considered** in construing statutory language [citation], liberal regard will be given to legislative intent so as to give effect to the salutary objects of the particular law. [Citations.] Zoning regulations are no exception to the foregoing principles. [Citation.]" (*Sechrist* v. *Municipal Court* (1976) 64 Cal. App.3d 737, 745 [134 Cal. Rptr. 733].) "In fact, a substantial amount of vagueness is permitted in California zoning ordinances...." (*Novi* v. *City of Pacifica* (1985) 169 Cal. App.3d 678, 682 [215 Cal. Rptr. 439] [antimonotony ordinance]; see also *Guinnane* v. *San Francisco City Planning Com.* (1989) 209 Cal. App.3d 732 [257 Cal. Rptr. 742] [residential character ordinance].)....

...we do not presume to know how expansively Carmel will interpret Ordinance No. 89-17. Although a very broad reading of "remuneration" or "bargained for consideration" **might lead to absurd applications,** as Carmel's attorney admitted, the legislative purpose is clearly to prohibit transient *commercial* use of residential property. ...

(10) Finally, we turn to plaintiffs' contention that Ordinance No. 89-17 violates their constitutional rights of substantive due process and equal protection. They argue first that the ordinance infringes upon their rights of freedom of association and of privacy guaranteed by the federal and state Constitutions. (See U.S. Const., 1st, 3d, 4th, 5th, & 9th Amends.; *Griswold* v. *Connecticut* (1965) 381 U.S. 479 [14 L.Ed.2d 510, 85 S.Ct. 1678]; Cal. [1596] Const., art. I, § 1; *White* v. *Davis* (1975) 13 Cal.3d 757 [120 Cal. Rptr. 94, 533 P.2d 222].)

Because these are fundamental rights (see *Griswold v. Connecticut, supra,* 381 U.S. at pp. 484-486 [14 L.Ed.2d at pp. 514-516] [privacy]; *N.A.A.C.P. v. Alabama* (1958) 357 U.S. 449, 460-461 [2 L.Ed.2d 1488, 1498-1499, 78 S.Ct. 1163] [association]), they contend **the ordinance is not presumed valid**, as would be the normal zoning ordinance. Rather, they maintain that **Carmel has the burden of demonstrating that the infringement upon constitutional rights is necessary to meet a compelling public need and that the ordinance is the least intrusive means of meeting that need**. (See *Moore v. East Cleveland* (1977) 431 U.S. 494, 499 [52 L.Ed.2d 531, 537-538, 97 S.Ct. 1932]; *Robbins v. Superior Court* (1985) 38 Cal.3d 199, 213 [211 Cal. Rptr. 398, 695 P.2d 695].)

Second, plaintiffs argue that even if the ordinance does not infringe upon fundamental rights, it still violates substantive due process and equal protection because it is **not rationally related to the goals sought to be achieved**. (See *Village of Belle Terre v. Boraas, supra,* 416 U.S. at p. 8 [39 L.Ed.2d at pp. 803-804]; *Roman Cath. etc. Corp. v. City of Piedmont* (1955) 45 Cal.2d 325, 331 [289 P.2d 438].)

We have already determined that the ordinance is rationally related to the stated goal. Carmel wishes to enhance and maintain the residential character of the R-1 District. Limiting transient commercial use of residential property for remuneration in the R-1 District addresses that goal. We have also concluded there is a rational basis for the 30-day cutoff and for the allowance of home occupations in the R-1 District despite the prohibitions contained in Ordinance No. 89-17....

In *Moore v. East Cleveland,* the United States Supreme Court struck down an ordinance limiting the occupancy of a single dwelling unit to members of a single "family"... When the government so intrudes ... "the usual judicial deference to the legislature is inappropriate." (*Moore v. East Cleveland, supra,* 431 U.S. at p. 499 [52 L.Ed.2d at p. 537].) .... **Review of Carmel's specific application and enforcement of the ordinance, if appropriate, must await another day**. (See *Euclid v. Ambler Co., supra,* 272 U.S. at pp. 395-397 [71 L.Ed. at pp. 313-315]; *People v. Wingo* (1975) 14 Cal.3d 169, 180 [121 Cal. Rptr. 97, 534 P.2d 1001] ["A statute valid on its face may be unconstitutionally applied."].)...The judgment is affirmed....A petition for a rehearing was denied November 5, 1991, and appellants' petition for review by the Supreme Court was denied January 8, 1992. ....

Ewing v. City of Carmel-By-The-Sea, 34 Cal.App.3d 1579 (6th Cir 1991)

2. Discussion of Low Income Housing and The Changes Required for Traditional Hotels

It is noted that the Santa Monica city council discussions appeared to weigh heavily the concerns regarding available low income housing and the complaints from the hotel workers union of the possible effect on hotel revenue and the effect on their jobs. The purpose of this discussion is to review basic economic factors that must be considered to resolve these issues.

Changed Circumstances, Vast Expansion of Tourism

For future years, it is foreseeable that hotels cannot keep pace with the tourist demand, as wealthy travelers from China, Korea, India, and Europe seek elegant lodging. Accordingly, the best strategy for a city is to simply accept the new economic circumstances, and promote short-term rentals as a way to stimulate the local economy.

Relevant evidence shows that the vast majority of short-term guest cause fewer problems than long-term residents. The tourist spends most of each day away from the place of lodging, fully occupied with spending at local restaurants, shopping and sightseeing. The net effect of tourist guests is substantial cash input to the local economy.

As a fundamental error, it is a mistake to stifle innovation through going too far with stringent regulations. Economic freedom is essential for natural forces to achieve a balance, without government interference. The required tax revenue to support city functions should come from increased economic activity, with funds from sales tax, property taxes, and selective excise taxes. Taxes on net income are designed by the federal and state governments with tax credits and deductions to stimulate the economy.

Lodging Tax is Ineffective and Inefficient

Typical <u>city</u> taxes and penalties, such as parking violations, lodging taxes, and excessive emergency vehicle fees, are inefficient because the net effect is to create opportunities to hire and pay more city employees to administer the newly created regulations.

The short term rental tax ordinance does <u>not</u> solve or improve either issue. The lodging tax and restriction of short-term rentals <u>damages the interests of both</u> low-income renters and the hotel workers. Lodging taxes are not efficient nor effective for increasing net city income because guests are price sensitive, so the reduction in revenue must be offset by using most of the hotel tax revenue for advertising to attract tourists. [1]

It is possible to design taxes so there is minimum interference with the economy.[2] As an alternative to a lodging tax, an <u>excise</u> tax could raise substantial funds with minimal controversy. For example, with voter approval, it may be feasible to increase the existing documentary transfer tax for real property sales, by simply increasing the current Santa Monica rate of 0.030 percent of sales to 2.00 percent of sales. Similarly, an excise tax could also be imposed on sales of securities, and on corporate mergers and acquisitions. As with broker commissions, typically 6% for houses and 1.5% to 3% for securities, the selling taxpayer would find the tax payment affordable due to the large amount of funds received from the sale.

---

[1] James Mak, Taxing Hotel Room Rentals in the U.S., *Journal of Travel Research*, July 1988, vol 27, No. 1, 10-15. Also see: S.J.Hiemstra and J.A. Ismail, Occupancy Taxes: No Free Lunch, *The Cornell Hotel and Restaurant Admin. Quarterly*, Vol 33, no. 5, Oct 1992, pp. 84-89.

[2] As stated by Jean Baptiste Cobert, Minister of Finance under King Louis XIV of France, "The art of taxation consists in so plucking the goose as to obtain the largest possible amount of feathers with the smallest possible amount of hissing"
http://thinkexist.com/quotation/the_art_of_taxation_consists_in_so_plucking_the/158604.html

Housing for Low Income Persons

As stated in various court decisions and economic studies, rent control and city regulation is <u>not</u> effective as a method to promote low rental prices for apartments or houses. Federal tax credits have provided some incentives for investors, but rents are still beyond the reach of many poor households without additional subsidy.[3]

Although it is typically asserted at city council hearings that short-term rentals increase the price of rent for apartments, the facts do <u>not</u> support this speculation. It is argued that short-term rental use reduces the available stock of apartments for long-term rentals. However, the large number of apartments and the small number of short-term rentals show that the effect on the local market is *de minimus*. Instead, apartment price for rent is driven by fundamental economic factors, such as inflation, construction cost, mortgage interest rate, location, quality, supply, and demand. Significantly, the primary factor in the price of rent is the local zoning and land-use constraints which inhibit land development for new residential use.

Based on informed city planning, there are several feasible methods that can result in improved housing and affordable prices. The first step is to <u>increase the income</u> of individuals. This increase can be in the form of a <u>bonus</u> paid from the city to the low income person, such as doubling the amount of income earned from employment or as contract labor. City funding for education and training can improve the earning potential of low income persons.

The next step is to provide <u>incentives to land development investors</u> and property owners. This incentive can be in the form of <u>free land</u> to qualified builders, provided that a reasonable proportion of the improvements are designed to be rented at bargain prices to low income persons. The free land can be

---

[3] Jean L. Cummings and Denise DiPasquale, The Low Income Housing Tax Credit, An Analysis of the First Ten Years, *Housing Policy Debate*, 10, 2, 251-307 (2010). Also see: Garvin A. Wood, Promoting the Supply of Low Income Housing, *Urban Policy and Research*, 19, 4, 425-440 (2007).

purchased by the city at market value in zones that are not now residential, or are areas already owned by the city. A city bond issue can pay for the acquisition cost of the land. An additional step is for the city to work closely with charity firms that are specialists in development and building of low income housing, such as *Habitat for Humanity (www.habitat.org).* Also, cities can work with banks to provide low interest loans for land development specialists. New ideas and improved methods can be applied to provide adequate housing for low income individuals. For example, the following arrangement would not require city expenditures or increased taxes. A city could provide loan guarantees to low income persons, who could then purchase a home with extra space that could be used for short term rentals. The extra income from rental would pay the mortgage, so that the renter is transformed to a property owner.

Hotel Income Issues

The basic reason that Airbnb rentals are rapidly becoming a preferred alternative to hotels is because Airbnb hosts typically offer a much higher quality lodging experience. By contrast, even five-star hotels fail to provide peace and quiet, a place away from congested city traffic, a private outside yard and patio with flowers, trees, and grass, high quality 600-thread 100% Egyptian cotton sheets, Smart water, premium towels, foam mattresses, a duvet with Austrian goose feathers, plus beverages and food in each room at no additional cost, and premium Khiel's, Fresh, and Neutrogena bath products. By contrast, a typical hotel has sensors on refrigerator contents, so a mere touch creates a charge on the hotel bill, the wifi is slow, the computer printer is in the lobby, and guests understands that it is not safe to leave a computer or other valuables in a hotel room. Recent studies show that Airbnb has only minor effect on business travelers, and results in pressure for lower hotel prices, which benefits hotels guests. [4]

---

[4] Zervas, Georgios and Proserpio, Davide and Byers, John, The Rise of the Sharing Economy: Estimating the Impact of Airbnb on the Hotel Industry (May 7, 2015). *Boston U. School of Management Research Paper* No. 2013-16. Also see: Kenneth T., Randall Sakamoto, & David Bank, *Short-Term Rentals and Impact on the Apartment Market. Berkeley, CA: Rosen Consulting Group, 2013.*
http://publicpolicy.airbnb.com/wp-content/uploads/2014/04/Short-TermRent.

People will pay for quality. However, hotels fail to create an atmosphere of excellence. It is common for the hotel employees to be underpaid and overworked, so that the interaction with guests lacks empathy and refined consideration. The low salaries must be supplemented by tips from guests, so that a guest lacks the freedom that would come from a fixed price for all services. Instead, as in a cafeteria or automat, the cumulative small charges result in a total price that is excessive. A substantial increase in salary for hotel workers and investment in top quality fixtures such as HansGrohe Rainshower bath fixtures, top quality lotions, and luxury furnishings such as 1926 Iranian rugs, solid oak hardwood floors, and oil paintings would result in higher total profits, resulting from improved guest relations and a more enjoyable stay.

In summary, each hotel <u>must search for new ways to improve the lodging experience</u>. For some hotels, this may require acquisition or building of separate high-quality homes in selected locations, so that a guest can select a villa at $950 a night instead of a small room for $525 a night. For specific locations, the rapid increase in house prices would make this strategy a good investment, even if there were minimal cash flow over a decade, based on the effect of inflation and increased demand in the local area, which would support triple the acquisition price on eventual sale of the villas after a decade of rental income. [5]

As shown by independent economic studies, short-term rentals are <u>not</u> a problem which needs government regulation. Instead, short-term rentals provide a practical <u>solution</u> to the requirement for economic stimulus and growth.

---

[5] Michael A. Cusumano, How Traditional Firms must Compete in the Sharing Economy, *Communications of the ACM*, 58,1, 32-34 (2015)

3. Discussion of Economic Damages

The purpose of this discussion is to document the analysis performed to determine the economic damages caused by the highly restrictive terms of the Santa Monica ordinance. The valuation date is June 15, 2015.

The Santa Monica transient occupancy tax was <u>not</u> the result of voter approval, as required for any new local tax by the California Constitution Article XIIIC. A finder of fact could determine that the definition of a home as a *de facto* hotel is an intentionally false classification. Also, a court could determine based on relevant law that the city must pay to the property owners <u>just compensation</u> for the economic damages caused by the ordinance, based on Fifth Amendment taking of property rights and substantive due process. The value of the property rights taken is the present value of cash flow not received by the hosts due to the terms of the ordinance, which prevent short term rentals for many current property owners.

A prudent investor would conclude that these factors demonstrate a substantial risk for investment in rental property in Santa Monica due to the risk and uncertainty regarding possible future court decisions. For purposes of calculation of lost income for the property owner income and lost tax revenue for the city, the analysis assumes two alternative events:

(1) The ordinance is promptly <u>deemed void,</u> so that there is <u>no decline</u> in income caused by the ordinance, so that all short term rentals continue as in the recent past.

(2) The ordinance is <u>enforced,</u> so that all multiple units and some of the single family units become <u>long term</u> rentals, which are rented only for time periods of 30 days or more. This would <u>substantially reduce</u> the monthly rental income and the total for the next decade for the rental properties.

Because of the <u>higher price</u> for short-term vs. long-term rentals, there is an increase in rental income for the property owners who rent short term. For

37

example, a small property that rents for $1,000 a month could receive $3,800 per month for a short term rental for a high-quality unit, with a price of $179 per night. Thus, the short term rental would result in gross rental income that is **3.8** times the long term rental.

However, to assure a conservative estimate of the lost income, a high vacancy rate and a lower nightly rental is assumed for the short-term rentals, with the result that the short-term rental is assumed to be only **2.123** times the long term rental price. For the example, the $1,000 monthly income is assumed to be only $2,123 per month for a short-term income. The multiplier of 0.471 (1 / 0.471= 2.123) is used to calculate long term income, based on the short term income. Each host is assumed to mitigate losses and city sanctions by promptly renting long term.

For Santa Monica, the calculations are based on data provided by Airdna (www.airdna.co) for Airbnb gross income for June 2015, the <u>annual</u> short term rental income for Airbnb rentals is $41,979,775. The revenue from HomeAway and other internet booking agents is estimated at $22,553,237 per year. Thus, the total income per year is:

Short Term Rental Income, per year

Airbnb short-term rental income	$41,979,776
HomeAway and other short term income	22,553,237
Total, short term rental income, Santa Monica	**$64,533,013**
Reduced income due to long term pricing, x 0.471	30,395,049
Loss of income per year, if ordinance enforced	**$34,137,964**

City tax income, at 14%, assuming voter approval of a tax

Tax income if <u>no restriction</u> of short term rental	$9,034,622
Tax income <u>with restriction</u> of short term rental	4,779,315
Loss of Santa Monica tax revenue, per year	**$4,255,307**

For future years, 2016 through 2026, the future gross rental income is assumed to increase at a rate slightly higher than inflation. After reduction of operating expenses, such as cleaning, maintenance, supplies and utilities, the result is net cash flow. The cash flow is calculated at the operating entity level so that corporate or personal income tax is not calculated. The present value of the future cash flow is based primary on the discount factor, which is the required yield for this type of investment risk.

This method of calculation of value is based on the method approved in the long chain of federal valuation cases which calculated the total value and the segregation of tangible assets and intangible assets based on the present value of future cash flow. See: *Newark Morning Ledger v. U.S.*, 507 U.S. 546 (1993).

The present value of rental income is based on a detailed calculation of future cash flow, based on foreseeable revenue and future operating expenses. To assure a conservative value, these calculations do not include the decline in asset value of the real property. Total market value for rental property is ordinarily based on the rental income, calculated either as a multiple of the gross income or as a detailed calculation of cash flow, including payment of all interest, taxes, and debts.

The market value is the equity value, which is defined as the market value of the assets, less the liabilities. The value of the rental operation is based on the market value of the underlying assets, including intangible assets. The value of intangible assets, such as goodwill, is based on a detailed calculation. The value of intangible assets is defined as the total value of the rental business, less the value of tangible assets. The total value of the business is the present value of future cash flow. For these facts, the interest, depreciation, and the value of the tangible assets are not included, because these additional factors have only a minor effect on total loss of income for these circumstances.

Present value. The present value reflects the discount in future receipt of cash due to the lost yield on a delayed receipt of cash. For example, $1.00 received today is worth $1.00, while the same $1.00 received 10 years in the future is worth only $0.43, because of the long delay and lost yield.

The current value of payment received in the future is determined by two factors, (1) the lapse of time, (2) the discount rate, which is the required yield. The discount factor is calculated based on the current required yield for investments with similar investment risk. For example, a discount factor of 9.185% results in a $1.00 being worth only $0.9770 after 6 months, and $0.7352 after 4.5 years, and $0.4340 after 9.5 years. This discount is based on the fact that $1.00 could be invested at 9.185% with a similar investment risk. The lost return on investment results in a reduction in the value of a delayed future payment.

Cash flow calculation. The cash flow calculation includes the amount received and the amount disbursed each year. The long-term residual value of the company is included in total company value. The required yield is derived from financial transactions with similar investment risks. Although the companies used to calculate the investment risk have business operations that are different from the subject hosts, the investment risk is sufficiently similar from the viewpoint of a prudent investor.

Critical factors. The following strategic factors significantly affect the value of the company:

1. <u>Revenue growth.</u> The revenue projection assumes increase in revenue due to gradual growth consistent with market growth and inflation. Although the future revenue is uncertain, and may be higher or lower, the projected growth rate assumes revenue growth that is slightly higher than inflation. Based on past performance and the market conditions, a prudent investor would assume only moderate future growth over the next ten years. Due to foreseeable economic factors, rapid future growth is not expected. Growth from future acquisitions is not included because the value of any future acquisition would be reflected in the price of any future acquisition.

2. <u>Cost control.</u> Careful control of future costs is required to assure that events conform to plans. Operating costs are assumed to be carefully controlled by the new investor, to allow improved future cash flow. Future operating costs are assumed to increase in proportion to the inflation rate and revenue.

3.   Required Yield.   The required yield is the cost of capital or return required for the investment risk, is the discount rate used to calculate the present value of future cash flow.

The investment risk for the company is calculated by reviewing the cost of capital for public firms that have similar investment risk. Several public firms were identified that were sufficiently similar to allow meaningful comparison of financial risk, as shown in the calculation of required yield. The public firms selected have sufficient trading volume to be selected for listing in Value Line. The Value Line data includes a calculation of beta, which is a comparison of stock value fluctuation as compared to the overall market. Data for public firms are used because detailed and accurate financial data for privately held firms are not available.   The required yield, or cost of capital, is the discount rate that is used to calculate the present value of future cash flow.   Investment risk is measured by the cost of capital for typical firms with similar investment risk. The cost of capital calculation includes review of the current risk-free interest rate, investment risk for the industry, and the proportion of debt versus equity in total company funding, termed the debt/capital ratio.

This valuation is based on a conservative, reasonable, and realistic calculation of the adjusted balance sheet, and is substantiated by the future cash flow.   The calculation methods used are widely recognized as accurate and appropriate for valuation of economic damages.

Calculation procedure.   This valuation of loss of income included the following procedures:
1.   **Review of background documents.** Relevant independent sources of information regarding market data, financial data, inflation factors, and interest rates were reviewed, such as:

Industry financial data from *Value Line*, Moody's Industrials, and *Ward's Business Directory of U.S. Private and Public Companies, Standard and Poor's*, and *Dun & Bradstreet.*

Data on interest rates and economic factors from the *Federal Reserve Bulletin, Economic Indicators*, and the *Economic Report of the President*.

Economic projections, including long-term inflation rates, such as *The Budget and Economic Outlook: FY 2015-2025*, Congressional Budget Office (CBO), January 2015, and *Forecast for California and the Nation*, UCLA Business Forecasting Project.

Detailed revenue and line-item expense data by industry from *Corporation Income Tax Returns* and *Partnership Income Tax Returns* from the Internal Revenue Service.

Detailed industry data from the *Census of Business* from the U.S. Dept. of Commerce.

2. Projection of future cash flow. The cash flow is based on a detailed calculation of foreseeable future revenue, expenses, and including future investments for capital expenditures. The revenue projection is based on foreseeable economic conditions, based on a review of prior revenue growth and our review of local circumstances. Although the 10-year projection is based on assumed average growth at a rate slightly higher than the rate of inflation, it is foreseeable that there will be fluctuation in sales volume from year to year, due to the cyclical nature of this business.

3. Projection of future operating costs. Future expenses were projected based on conservative assumptions. Accordingly, primary emphasis was based on recent actual expense ratios. Separate calculations were made for each major element of cost as related to revenue. As appropriate, future costs are based on a line-item review of recent historical costs as related to revenue. Future costs are assumed to reflect prudent cost control.

4. Calculation of loss of income. The total amount of the loss of income is calculated as the present value of cash flow. The discount factor is the <u>required yield</u>, termed the cost of capital, for the specific operations, based on the cost of capital for the industry plus an additional discount for small financial size and risk for the specific circumstances.

5. Scrutiny of valuation results. The sensitivity to various changes in assumptions was tested by preparing alternative cash flow projections. These were based on a wide range of specific assumptions derived from a review of economic forecasts, industry circumstances, relevant market conditions and cost trends within the firm. Annual revenue growth and projected operating costs were found to be critical factors affecting equity value. The amount of future expenses as compared to revenue was found to be a major factor affecting future cash flow. Significantly, future revenue is limited by competitive rental rates and only a few operating costs are subject to the discretion and control of the owner. The calculations reflect assumptions that are understood to be *reasonable*, under the specific circumstances that are foreseeable for this type of operation.

The typical calculation issues are discussed in court cases and reference books in tax law, finance, and economics. Traditional methods, such as comparison of financial ratios, are understood to be only approximate. With the cash flow method, the sensitivity of the result to underlying calculation assumptions may be tested through iteration. The cash flow calculation method allows focus on the significant and sensitive valuation factors.

Just Compensation, Loss of Income
Short Term Rentals, Santa Monica
Fiscal Years Ending Jun 15

Planning Factors	FY Jun 15 Actual 2015		Estimated 2016	Projected 2017
Inflation, CPI-U, year to year	1.49%		1.57%	2.80%
Growth in total revenue, % year			4.50%	4.21%
Growth in outlays, %/yr			3.57%	4.80%
Date of valuation **15-Jun-15**				

INCOME

Revenue, if ordinance not enforced

Airbnb	$ 41,979,776	$	43,868,866	$ 45,717,746
HomeAway, other	22,553,237		23,568,133	24,561,426
Total, if ordinance not enforced	**$ 64,533,013**	**$**	**67,436,999**	**$ 70,279,172**
Revenue, if Ordinance enforced	30,395,049		31,762,827	33,101,490
Total, Loss of Income	**$ 34,137,964**	**$**	**35,674,172**	**$ 37,177,682**

EXPENSES for short term rentals

Cleaning, maintenance, 80/521	$ 5,241,914	$	5,477,800	$ 5,708,665
Supplies, 35/521	2,293,337		2,396,537	2,497,541
Utilities, 8/521	524,191		547,780	570,867
Subtotal, Operating costs	**$ 8,059,443**	**$**	**8,422,117**	**$ 8,777,073**
Administrative, operating costs	1,053		1,176	1,209
Total, Expenses	**$ 8,060,496**	**$**	**8,423,294**	**$ 8,778,282**
Income, before tax	**$ 26,077,469**	**$**	**27,250,878**	**$ 28,399,400**
Income tax, at business entity level	-		-	-
Income after tax	**$ 26,077,469**	**$**	**27,250,878**	**$ 28,399,400**

CASH FLOW

Income after tax	$ 26,077,469	$	27,250,878	$ 28,399,400
Elapsed years				1.00
Lapse of time, mid-year				0.50
Discount factor 9.837%				0.9542
Discounted cash flow				$ 27,097,874
Loss of Income, present value	**$207,285,190**			

IMPACT ON ECONOMY

Loss of Income for property owners	**$207,285,190**
Operating expenses not made	109,140,256
Total Local Outlays not made	**$316,425,446**
Economic Muliplier **2.30**	2.30
Total Economic Loss to Local Area	**$727,778,526**

Just Compensation, Loss of Income
Short Term Rentals, Santa Monica
Fiscal Years Ending Jun 15

Planning Factors		2018	2019	2020
Inflation, CPI-U, year to year		2.80%	2.80%	2.80%
Growth in total revenue, % year		3.99%	3.74%	3.34%
Growth in outlays, %/yr		4.80%	4.80%	4.80%
Date of valuation	**15-Jun-15**			
INCOME				
Revenue, if ordinance not enforced				
Airbnb		$ 47,543,968	$ 49,324,281	$ 50,973,961
HomeAway, other		25,542,547	26,499,003	27,385,278
Total, if ordinance not enforced		**$ 73,086,515**	**$ 75,823,284**	**$ 78,359,239**
Revenue, if Ordinance enforced		34,423,749	35,712,767	36,907,202
Total, Loss of Income		**$ 38,662,767**	**$ 40,110,517**	**$ 41,452,038**
EXPENSES for short term rentals				
Cleaning, maintenance, 80/521		$ 5,936,701	$ 6,159,005	$ 6,364,996
Supplies, 35/521		2,597,307	2,694,564	2,784,686
Utilities, 8/521		593,670	615,900	636,500
Subtotal, Operating costs		**$ 9,127,678**	**$ 9,469,470**	**$ 9,786,182**
Administrative, operating costs		1,243	1,278	1,314
Total, Expenses		**$ 9,128,921**	**$ 9,470,748**	**$ 9,787,495**
Income, before tax		**$ 29,533,845**	**$ 30,639,770**	**$ 31,664,542**
Income tax, at business entity level		-	-	-
Income after tax		**$ 29,533,845**	**$ 30,639,770**	**$ 31,664,542**
CASH FLOW				
Income after tax		$ 29,533,845	$ 30,639,770	$ 31,664,542
Elapsed years		2.00	3.00	4.00
Lapse of time, mid-year		1.50	2.50	3.50
Discount factor	9.837%	0.8687	0.7909	0.7201
Discounted cash flow		$ 25,656,546	$ 24,233,482	$ 22,801,093
Loss of Income, present value				

IMPACT ON ECONOMY

  Loss of Income for property owners

  Operating expenses not made

  Total Local Outlays not made

  Economic Muliplier   **2.30**

Total Economic Loss to Local Area

Just Compensation, Loss of Income
Short Term Rentals, Santa Monica
Fiscal Years Ending Jun 15

Planning Factors		2021	2022	2023
Inflation, CPI-U, year to year		2.80%	2.80%	2.80%
Growth in total revenue, % year		2.94%	2.54%	2.14%
Growth in outlays, %/yr		4.80%	4.80%	4.80%
Date of valuation	**15-Jun-15**			
INCOME				
Revenue, if ordinance not enforced				
Airbnb		$ 52,474,920	$ 53,810,176	$ 54,964,167
HomeAway, other		28,191,654	28,909,008	29,528,979
Total, if ordinance not enforced		**$ 80,666,574**	**$ 82,719,183**	**$ 84,493,146**
Revenue, if Ordinance enforced		37,993,956	38,960,735	39,796,272
Total, Loss of Income		**$ 42,672,618**	**$ 43,758,448**	**$ 44,696,874**
EXPENSES for short term rentals				
Cleaning, maintenance, 80/521		$ 6,552,417	$ 6,719,147	$ 6,863,244
Supplies, 35/521		2,866,683	2,939,627	3,002,669
Utilities, 8/521		655,242	671,915	686,324
Subtotal, Operating costs		**$ 10,074,342**	**$ 10,330,689**	**$ 10,552,237**
Administrative, operating costs		1,351	1,388	1,427
Total, Expenses		**$ 10,075,692**	**$ 10,332,078**	**$ 10,553,664**
Income, before tax		**$ 32,596,925**	**$ 33,426,370**	**$ 34,143,210**
Income tax, at business entity level		-	-	-
Income after tax		**$ 32,596,925**	**$ 33,426,370**	**$ 34,143,210**
CASH FLOW				
Income after tax		$ 32,596,925	$ 33,426,370	$ 34,143,210
Elapsed years		5.00	6.00	7.00
Lapse of time, mid-year		4.50	5.50	6.50
Discount factor	9.837%	0.6556	0.5969	0.5434
Discounted cash flow		$ 21,370,329	$ 19,951,517	$ 18,554,240
Loss of Income, present value				

IMPACT ON ECONOMY

Loss of Income for property owners

Operating expenses not made

Total Local Outlays not made

Economic Muliplier **2.30**

Total Economic Loss to Local Area

Just Compensation, Loss of Income
Short Term Rentals, Santa Monica
Fiscal Years Ending Jun 15

Planning Factors		2024	2025	2026
Inflation, CPI-U, year to year		2.80%	2.80%	2.80%
Growth in total revenue, % year		1.74%	1.34%	0.94%
Growth in outlays, %/yr		4.80%	4.80%	4.80%
Date of valuation	**15-Jun-15**			
INCOME				
Revenue, if ordinance not enforced				
Airbnb		$ 55,923,050	$ 56,674,969	$ 57,210,298
HomeAway, other		30,044,129	30,448,091	30,735,691
Total, if ordinance not enforced		**$ 85,967,179**	**$ 87,123,060**	**$ 87,945,989**
Revenue, if Ordinance enforced		40,490,542	41,034,961	41,422,561
Total, Loss of Income		**$ 45,476,638**	**$ 46,088,099**	**$ 46,523,428**
EXPENSES for short term rentals				
Cleaning, maintenance, 80/521		$ 6,982,977	$ 7,076,867	$ 7,143,713
Supplies, 35/521		3,055,052	3,096,129	3,125,374
Utilities, 8/521		698,298	707,687	714,371
Subtotal, Operating costs		**$ 10,736,327**	**$ 10,880,684**	**$ 10,983,458**
Administrative, operating costs		1,467	1,508	1,551
Total, Expenses		**$ 10,737,795**	**$ 10,882,192**	**$ 10,985,009**
Income, before tax		**$ 34,738,843**	**$ 35,205,907**	**$ 35,538,420**
Income tax, at business entity level		-	-	-
Income after tax		**$ 34,738,843**	**$ 35,205,907**	**$ 35,538,420**
CASH FLOW				
Income after tax		$ 34,738,843	$ 35,205,907	$ 35,538,420
Elapsed years		8.00	9.00	10.00
Lapse of time, mid-year		7.50	8.50	9.50
Discount factor	9.837%	0.4948	0.4504	0.4101
Discounted cash flow		$ 17,187,247	$ 15,858,373	$ 14,574,489
Loss of Income, present value				

IMPACT ON ECONOMY

  Loss of Income for property owners

  Operating expenses not made

    Total Local Outlays not made

    Economic Muliplier   **2.30**

  Total Economic Loss to Local Area

Just Compensation, Loss of Income
Short Term Rentals, Santa Monica
Fiscal Years Ending Jun 15

	Total
Planning Factors	2016-2026
Inflation, CPI-U, year to year	
Growth in total revenue, % year	
Growth in outlays, %/yr	
Date of valuation **15-Jun-15**	
INCOME	
Revenue, if ordinance not enforced	
Airbnb	$ 568,486,401
HomeAway, other	305,413,940
Total, if ordinance not enforced	$ 873,900,341
Revenue, if Ordinance enforced	411,607,061
Total, Loss of Income	**$ 462,293,280**
EXPENSES for short term rentals	
Cleaning, maintenance, 80/521	$ 70,985,532
Supplies, 35/521	31,056,170
Utilities, 8/521	7,098,553
Subtotal, Operating costs	**$ 109,140,256**
Administrative, operating costs	14,914
Total, Expenses	**$ 109,155,170**
Income, before tax	**$ 353,138,110**
Income tax, at business entity level	-
Income after tax	**$ 353,138,110**
CASH FLOW	
Income after tax	$ 353,138,110
Elapsed years	
Lapse of time, mid-year	
Discount factor 9.837%	
Discounted cash flow	**$ 207,285,190**
Loss of Income, present value	
IMPACT ON ECONOMY	
Loss of Income for property owners	**$ 207,285,190**
Operating expenses not made	$ -
Total Local Outlays not made	**$ 316,425,446**
Economic Muliplier **2.30**	2.30
Total Economic Loss to Local Area	**$ 727,778,526**

Just Compensation, Loss of Income
Short Term Rentals, Santa Monica
Fiscal Years Ending Jun 15

Planning Factors <u>Calculation Factors</u>

Inflation, CPI-U, year to year
Growth in total revenue, % year
Growth in outlays, %/yr
Date of valuation   **15-Jun-15**

INCOME

Revenue, if ordinance not enforced

  Airbnb   based on detailed data from Airdna

  HomeAway, other   estimated based on Airbnb revenue

Total, if ordinance not enforced

Revenue, if Ordinance enforced   0.471 x revenue if no ordinance

Total, Loss of Income

EXPENSES for short term rentals

Cleaning, maintenance, 80/521   0.153550864 x revenue if no ordinance
Supplies, 35/521   0.067178503 x revenue if no ordinance
Utilities, 8/521   0.015355086 x revenue if no ordinance

Subtotal, Operating costs

Administrative, operating costs   0.010526316 x revenue if no ordinance

Total, Expenses

Income, before tax

Income tax, at business entity level   Sch E, Sch. C, S Corp or partnership assumed

Income after tax   Gross rental income less operating expenses

CASH FLOW

Income after tax
Elapsed years
Lapse of time, mid-year
Discount factor   9.837% required yield, for investment with similar risk
Discounted cash flow

Loss of Income, present value   present value of future cash flow

IMPACT ON ECONOMY

  Loss of Income for property owners   Loss of income for owners over 10 years

  Operating expenses not made   Expenses not made by property owners

Total Local Outlays not made

  Economic Muliplier   **2.30** Macroeconomic factor, typical range 1.5 to 4.0

Total Economic Loss to Local Area

5. *Discussion of the Required Investment Yield*

The following is a detailed discussion of the <u>required yield</u>, which is used as a factor for the calculation of the present value of the future cash flow for short term rental of real property in Santa Monica. The valuation date is June 15, 2015.

The required yield on the valuation date is based on the *Federal Reserve Statistical Release H.15*. The required yield is a significant factor for calculation of the investment risk for the partial interest discount and for the valuation of corporate equity. The required yield is the discount factor that determines the present value of future cash flow. The stock market for publicly-traded shares provides measurements on investment risk, based on recent transactions. The investment risk varies with the financial structure and stock market fluctuations. Publicly-traded securities transactions are used because the data covers a wide range of transactions, and the underlying financial structure and performance is based on audited financial statements.

The specific industry selected for similar investment risk is the Real Estate Investment Trusts (REITs). Although company operations are different, REITs are selected because the investment risk is moderate, with stable growth and only moderate fluctuation. By contrast, alternative industries typically reflect higher investment risks, volatile growth, and fluctuation of value as compared to an investment in real property. Accordingly, this required yield is conservative.

The required yield depends on the interest rate, investment risk and the capital structure. The interest rate is based on the risk-free rate for government bonds and corporate bonds on the valuation date. The investment risk is measured by beta, which compares industry stock price fluctuation to total market fluctuation. The capital structure, the proportion of debt, affects the cost of capital because the cost of debt is typically lower than the cost of equity.

Although risk-free investment such as a federal government bond offer minimum investment risk, the expected yield is much lower than the long term return from corporate stock. However, the higher potential yield for corporate stock involves higher risk. This balance between risk and return is demonstrated by the actual investments made in the securities market. The required yield depends on the industry risk and the relationship between debt and equity for the industry. The following discussion describes a widely-accepted method for calculation of the required yield, based on a specified level of risk and debt structure.

Investment risk varies with each type of industry. For a relatively stable industry, the real estate investment trusts (REITs) provides a reliable standard, because the returns depend primarily on the capital market and the economic trends, with minimum impact from technology changes. Accordingly, this industry is selected to represent required yield for a wide range of long term investments.

The required yield is based on different decision criteria as compared to the Treasury regulations that specify the applicable interest rate for other transactions, such as some types of debt instruments. For example, the IRS uses the applicable federal funds rate (AFR) to determine the imputed interest income for debt instruments in certain situations, such as tax shelters, 26 USC §1274. Similarly, the IRS may impute interest under the AFR for certain sales of property, 26 USC §483. By contrast, the required yield specifies the return on investment that a prudent investor would require, based on the risk-free return plus a risk premium that allows adequate compensation for the investment risk.

The cost of capital is the required return on investment; it is the discount rate used to calculate the present value of future cash flow. Adjustments are made in the cost of capital to reflect added risk due to small financial size, lack of a proprietary position, or other factors that indicate a high financial risk. From the viewpoint of a prudent investor, a proposed investment must offer a yield higher than the cost of capital.

Overview

The cost of capital is based on separate calculations for the cost of debt and the cost of equity. The cost of debt is calculated after tax, to reflect the effects of the interest deduction. The cost of equity includes the effect of leverage on beta and an assumed optimum industry debt/capital ratio. The cost of equity is calculated as the risk free rate plus levered premium:

$(R_f + (P_e \times Beta))$

R_f = Risk free rate, cost of debt

P_e = Equity risk premium, from Ibbotson data

Beta = Risk factor, derived from stock market data

The calculation method for the cost of equity uses the risk free rate plus a premium for risk. This calculation method for the cost of capital is documented in a widely-accepted financial textbook[1].

Selection of Comparable Firms

Reasonable values for beta and the debt/capital ratio are based on a review of the capital structure for comparable firms in the relevant industry. Diligent care was taken to assure that the selection of the specific firms used for comparables are representative of the type of firm that represent similar investment risk based on industry characteristics.

Risk associated with the future income stream may be measured by The cost of capital calculation requires a measurement of beta for the relevant industry. Beta is the calculated value based on the amount of stock price fluctuation as compared to the entire stock market over a period of years. The public companies listed in *Value Line* have sufficient trading volume to allow a reliable and accurate calculation of beta, which is an accepted measure of the

---

[1] J. Fred Weston and Thomas E. Copeland, *Managerial Finance*, 9th Edition (The Dryden Press, 1992), pp. 606-623.

volatility of the selected stock as compared to the fluctuations in the entire stock market. A small financial size results in higher financial risk, calculated at a premium of 3.05 points. This small investment premium is calculated based on the difference in the cost of capital between large and small companies over a period of many years.

Market Risk Premium

The premium for risk is a sensitive factor in the cost of capital calculation. A risk premium is used for calculation of the cost of equity, derived from historical data from Ibbotson for a 10-year holding period. The premium for market risk varies with the holding period, as demonstrated by data tabulated by Ibbotson[2]. The risk premium for different holding periods is summarized below, using data from 1926-1992:

	Holding period		
	20 year	10 year	5 year
Common stocks	10.53	10.39	9.90
Less, long-term gov't. bonds	3.50	4.19	4.55
Equity premium	7.02	6.20	5.35
Small stock premium	3.52	3.55	3.84

The equity premium is the additional yield required by a prudent investor for an investment in stock instead of long-term government bonds. As shown above, using 1926-1992 data, the equity premium was 6.20, and the small stock premium was 3.55. However, using more recent data including the 1926-1996 period, the equity premium is 5.95 percent and the small stock premium is 3.05 percent.

Discussion of the Calculation Method

The cost of capital is significant because it is the discount rate used to calculate the present value of future cash flow. The cost of capital is the return required to compensate an investor for use of investment funds. Capital is the amount of funds required to operate a business firm; capital is defined as

---

[2]*Stocks, Bonds, Bills, and Inflation*, 1996 Yearbook. Chicago: Ibbotson Associates, 1996, pp. 43-47.

liabilities plus equity. Liabilities are the debts of the firm, including accounts payable, short-term debt and long-term debt. Equity is assets minus liabilities. The cost of capital is the required rate of return for the specific investment and is intended to reflect the basic cost of funds plus the investment risk associated with the specific investment of the funds.

The primary factor that determines the required rate of return is the risk. Increased risk requires increased compensation; thus, the greater the degree to which the price and returns of a security fluctuate, the greater the financial risk. U.S. government securities are considered to be free of risk of default for timely payment of principal or interest. The 10-year Treasury Bond is used to match the holding period for the investment.

The required rate of return is based on two key factors: 1) the expected rates for risk-free financial instruments as measured by government bond rates whose maturity approximates the expected duration of the income stream; and 2) the perceived risk of the income stream. The yield to maturity of the bond is calculated on the basis of its market price and the time remaining until its maturity. The risk premium is the amount that an investor requires above the long term risk-free government rate. The amount of the risk premium varies with the holding period. The risk premium for a 61-year holding period, from 1926 through 1987, is 7.4 percent, as determined by Ibbotson & Sinquefield.[1] A 10-year holding period was assumed for the subject investment. Thus, based on detailed calculation using a 10-year holding period, the risk premium used in our calculations reflected the calculated figure for a 10 year holding period, using data for 1926-1995.

The risk premium was based on common stock total returns versus long-term government bond yields. Common stock return includes the effect of dividends, inflation, and growth in the economy. The risk premium for this industry is not published by Ibbotson. The required rate of return is expressed as the weighted average cost of capital. The cost of capital calculation is based on a weighted average of the component costs for debt and equity.

---

[1] Roger G. Ibbotson & Rex A. Sinquefield, *Stocks, Bonds, Bills & Inflation: Historical Returns (1926-1987)* (Homefield, IL: Dow-Jones Irwin, 1989), p. 77.

The cost of capital and its components are a function of the financing sources' debt and equity ratios. Without corporate taxes, the weighted average cost of capital does not vary with the debt/equity ratio, given specific assumptions.[2] With taxes, the weighted average cost of capital declines with increasing debt to reflect the deduction effect of interest. There are four basic types of financing available for an investment. These include common stock, preferred stock, debt, and retained earnings. Each of these four basic types have possible variations, such as debt which is convertible to stock or stock that is convertible to debt; options; variations in preference to assets on liquidation; and voting rights. Similarly, debt also covers a broad range, from unsecured accounts payable to long-term secured debt. For the purposes of analysis, these multiple financing types are reduced to two basic types--debt and equity. Calculation of the weighted average cost of capital requires an analysis of the debt/equity structure and a determination of the cost of debt and the cost of equity. The cost of debt must also reflect an adjustment for the effect of income taxes. Thus, the determination of an appropriate discount rate requires identifying three primary variables: 1) the proportion of debt vs. equity 2) the after tax cost of debt, and 3) the cost of equity.

The following shows the calculation method:

$$Discount\ Rate\ =\ (K_d \times S_d) + (K_e \times S_e)$$

where,

$$K_d = the\ cost\ of\ debt,\ after\ tax$$

$$K_e = the\ cost\ of\ equity$$

$$S_d = percentage\ debt$$

$$S_e = percentage\ of\ stockholders'\ equity$$

---

[2]Modigliani, Franco, and Miller, Merton H., "The Cost of Capital, Corporation Finance and the Theory of Investment," *American Economic Review*, 48 (June 1958), pp. 261-297, and J. Fred Weston and Thomas E. Copeland, *Management Finance*, 8th Edition (The Dryden Press, 1989), p. 619.

In summary, the *weighted average cost of capital* is the cost of debt times the proportion of debt, plus the cost of equity times the proportion of equity. The cost of capital calculation involves empirical data analysis combined with seasoned judgment based on experience.

Proportion of Debt vs. Equity

The determination of an appropriate capital structure is a sensitive factor in the cost of capital. The capital structure is the proportion of debt as compared to the proportion of equity. The average debt/capital ratio is measured for selected comparable firms. Then, this average is compared to typical debt/capital ratios found to be efficient for a wider range of firms. The optimum ratio depends on the type of firm; leasing firms exhibit high

Cost of Debt

We used the following procedure to calculate the cost of debt:

1. The average corporate debt rate is calculated. This is the arithmetic average of the rate for seasoned corporate bonds with a Moody's credit rating of Aaa and Baa.

2. To assure that the required yield calculations are consistent with the circumstances for the comparable companies, the required yield is calculated for an assumed investor, who is a C corporation which would file a consolidated tax return, and is located in a state that has corporate state tax. The tax rate is calculated for the combined effect of state and federal income tax. State tax is assumed to be 11 percent, reflecting the highest corporate rate for California. The federal tax rate is 35 percent for tax years beginning after January 1, 1993, Code 11(b)(1), 1993 Act Section 13221(a). State tax paid is a deduction for federal tax returns. For these assumptions, the combined income tax rate is 42.15 percent. The cost of debt is adjusted to reflect the after-tax cost because interest is a tax deduction.

3. The after-tax cost of debt is based on a combined marginal tax rate of 42.15 percent, which represents a Federal corporate rate of 35 percent and an average state tax rate of 11 percent.

For example, if the pretax interest rate is 7.905 percent, the after-tax cost of debt is:

$$K_d \quad = \quad K(1-t)$$

where,

K_d = *after-tax cost of debt*
K = *pretax yield (average corporate bond rate, plus premium)*
t = *marginal tax rate, or 42.15%*

The cost of debt was derived by using the unweighted average of corporate bonds rated A and Baa for the valuation date, as listed in the *Federal Reserve Statistical Release*, Report H.15. The Baa rating reflects higher risk than the Aaa rating, which is the highest rating for corporate bonds. The Aaa rating has minimum risk of default and foreseeable adequate cash flow to repay debt. In the event of adverse economic conditions, this deficiency could suggest susceptibility to impairment of payments at some time in the future.

Cost of Equity

The cost of equity is defined as the minimum rate of return that an investment must earn on the equity-financed portion of its capital to leave the market price of its stock unchanged. The cost of equity requires a detailed calculation including risk-free rate and the risk premium. For the risks that are involved with a specific investment, investors require higher returns. This relationship between risk and return is expressed in the following equation:

$$R_i = R_f + R_p$$

where,

R_i = *risk for the investment, total*

R_f = *risk-free rate*

R_p = *risk premium*

The capital asset pricing model measures only systematic risk, which is that part of a security's risk that cannot be eliminated by diversification because it is related to the movement of the stock market. The assumption is that investors can easily eliminate investment-specific risk by properly diversifying portfolios, but are not compensated for bearing unsystematic risk.

The capital asset pricing model uses *beta* to measure the extent to which the returns on a given investment move with the stock market as a whole. *Beta* is a gauge of a security's volatility in comparison with the volatility of the entire stock market. The following procedure was used to calculate the cost of equity:

1. The industry volatility factor, beta, was tabulated for each firm, as reported by *Value Line*.

2. The debt/capital ratio was calculated for each firm. Capital is defined as the total of equity plus liabilities. Debt is capital minus equity. Thus, debt is defined to include all types of debt, including both current and long-term debt.

3. An unlevered beta was calculated for each firm to reflect the effect of the debt/capital ratio for each firm on the reported beta.

4. A levered beta was calculated for the industry to reflect the industry average optimum debt/capital ratio. The levered beta represents the cost of capital for a prudent corporate investor, assuming an efficient proportion of debt.

5. The risk premium was calculated. The risk premium is the equity risk premium times beta. The equity risk premium is calculated as 5.95 percent, using a 10-year holding period, based on 1926-1995 data. Levered beta is used in the calculation, to include the effect of capital structure on beta.

6. The risk-free rate was added to the risk premium to derive the cost of equity. The risk-free rate is the short term rate for government debt, defined as the rate for a 10-year U.S. Government bond.

Because beta for each investment reflects the capital structure of each investment, we computed an unlevered beta from the available data to reflect the industry average risk, adjusted for leverage.

The following calculation is used to compensate for the degree of leverage in the comparable companies:

$$B_u = \frac{B_l}{1 + (1 - t)\,(d/c)}$$

where,

B_u =*unlevered beta*
B_l =*levered beta*
t =*income tax, marginal rate, 42.15 percent*
d =*total debt*
c =*capital, total debt plus equity*

Separate calculations were made for each investment to unlever the beta, using the debt/capital ratio for each investment and a 42.15 percent tax rate. The unlevered beta is a measure of risk corrected for the specific capital structure of each firm. The calculations result in *unlevered beta of* a slightly *lower* volatility as compared to the entire stock market. This volatility figure, however, must be adjusted to reflect the capital structure for the investment, to allow for higher risk associated with higher debt. The levered beta includes the risk of the specific capital structure.

The risk of the income stream for a specific industry is determined by measuring the level of risk exhibited by typical firms in the industry. Beta is a measurement of the variability or volatility of the company stock with respect to the entire stock market and is reported by *Value Line*. The *Value Line* beta calculation is based on weekly data over a five-year period, comparing fluctuation in the specific stock to fluctuation in the entire stock market. Stocks with betas greater than 1.00 tend to have a higher degree of systematic risk and a stronger sensitivity to market swings. Conversely, stocks with betas less than 1.00 tend to rise and fall by a lesser percentage than the market.

The next step is to combine the optimal capital structure with the industry average unlevered beta to obtain the levered beta (B_l) used to calculate the cost of equity. The levered beta reflects the additional equity premium that equity investors would require to compensate for the risks inherent in the industry.

The levered beta is calculated as follows:

$$B_u[1 + (1 - t)(d/c)] = B_l$$

The risk/expected return relationship that we derive by applying the capital asset pricing model is known as the security market line. The risk premium is measured by beta multiplied by the equity premium. The equity premium is calculated from Ibbotson data, comparing common stock with long term government bonds, over a 10-year holding period:

$$K_e = R_f + B(P_e)$$

where,

K_e = *cost of equity*

R_f = *the risk-free rate*

B = *beta, industry levered*

P_e = *Equity premium, based on stock vs. gov't. bond yield*

The risk premium represents the additional return necessary to compensate for the increased risk of an average stock market equity investment compared to the risk-free government security. The equity risk premium varies with the holding period. Data calculated by Ibbotson and Sinquefield[3] indicated that equity investors require a 7.4 percent premium, based on a 61-year investment horizon. For a 10-year investment horizon, the risk premium is calculated at 5.95 percent, based on 1926-1995 data. For the risk-free rate, we used the interest rate for 10-year Treasury Bonds as reported by the Federal Reserve Bulletin.

This cost of equity includes an adjustment for the assumed optimum capital structure and the effect of the capital structure on beta.

---

[3]Roger G. Ibbotson and Rex A. Sinquefield, *Stocks, Bonds, Bills and Inflation: Historical Returns* (1926-1987), (Homefield, IL: Dow Jones-Irwin, 1989), p. 77.

Summary, The Cost of Capital

After computing the cost of debt and the cost of equity, the weighted average cost of capital is show from the following equation:

$$WACC = (K_d \; x \; S_d) + (K_e \; x \; S_e)$$

where

$WACC$	=	*weighted average cost of capital*
K_d	=	*cost of debt, after tax*
S_d	=	*proportion of debt*
K_e	=	*cost of equity*
S_e	=	*proportion of equity*

An additional 3.05 points were added to the industry figure to reflect additional risk due to small financial size, as contrasted to large public companies used for calculation purposes. This additional premium is the small stock premium for a 10 year holding period, as calculated from Ibbotson data. An additional premium is added to reflect the investment risk for the specific circumstances.

The weighted average cost of capital is intended to reflect the investment risk demonstrated by the financial markets for the industry, with adjustment to reflect the additional risk for the specific investment. The required yield is the discount rate that is used to derive the present value of future cash flow, based on projected income and expenses.

COST OF CAPITAL CALCULATION

Real Estate Investment Firms, Residential

COST OF EQUITY (Ke)

Industry Volatility Factor, Beta

BRE Properties	1.05	Data for 2012 is from Value Line, Apr 13, 2012
Equity Residential	1.10	Data for 2012 is from Value Line, Apr 13, 2012
Realty Income Corp.	0.90	Data for 2012 is from Value Line, Apr 13, 2012
Washington REIT	1.00	Data for 2012 is from Value Line, Apr 13, 2012
UDR Inc,	1.05	Data for 2012 is from Value Line, Apr 13, 2012
Federal Realty	1.10	Data for 2012 is from Value Line, Apr 13, 2012
Kimko Realty Corp.	1.30	Data for 2012 is from Value Line, Apr 13, 2012
Beta, industry average	1.07	Unweighted average of above

Debt/Capital ratio

BRE Properties	32.188%	Calculated as (total debt / capital)
Equity Residential	64.813%	
Realty Income Corp.	31.797%	
Washington REIT	37.329%	
UDR Inc,	42.589%	
Federal Realty	43.706%	
Kimko Realty Corp.	37.432%	
Debt/Capital Ratio,average	45.189%	Weighted mean, total debt/capital
Debt/Capital Ratio, optimum	53.110%	Assumed higher than typical debt for financial leverage.

Beta, Unlevered

BRE Properties	0.885	(Beta)/((1+(1-tax rate) x (debt/capital ratio)))
Equity Residential	0.800	
Realty Income Corp.	0.760	
Washington REIT	0.822	
UDR Inc,	0.842	
Federal Realty	0.878	
Kimko Realty Corp.	1.069	
Beta, Unlevered, Industry Average	0.865	Average, arithmetic mean, of above
Beta, Levered, Industry Average	1.091	(Unlevered Beta, avg.) x (1+(1-tax) x (debt/capital, avg.))
Beta, Levered, Assumed Optimum	1.131	(Unlevered Beta, avg.) x (1+(1-tax) x (debt/capital, opt.))

Risk-Free Rate, short-term (Rf)

Risk Free rate, Gov't Bonds, 10 y	2.360%	Fed. Reserve Statistical Release, H.15, Jun 15, 2015
Beta, Levered, Industry Optimum	1.131	Derived, from calculations above.
Equity premium (Pe)	5.950%	Input, from Ibbotson data, 10 yr. hold, 1926-1995
Premium, Levered	6.730%	Beta (levered optimum) times equity premium
Total, cost of equity (Ke)	9.090%	Risk free rate plus levered premium

COST OF DEBT (Kd)

Corporate bonds, seasoned, Aaa	4.190%	Fed. Reserve Statistical Release, H.15, Jun 15, 2015
Corporate bonds, seasoned, Baa	5.090%	Fed. Reserve Statistical Release, H.15, Jun 15, 2015
Average, corporate debt rate	4.640%	Average, arithmetic mean, of above
Tax rate, state and federal	42.150%	Combined rate, 11% state, 35% federal
After tax factor (1-tax rate)	57.850%	(1 - tax rate)
Cost of debt, after tax(Kd)	2.684%	Cost of debt times after tax factor
Total Cost of Capital	**9.837%**	Weighted average, premium, small size, city risk.

67

COST OF CAPITAL CALCULATION
Real Estate Investment Firms, Residential

WEIGHTED AVERAGE COST OF CAPITAL

	Cost After Tax	Percent of Capital	Weighted Average	
Debt	2.684%	53.11%	1.426%	Debt/capital ratio is asssumed optimum
Equity	9.090%	46.89%	4.262%	Equity % of capital is (1- debt %)
Subtotal, cost of capital			5.688%	(debt cost x % debt)+(equity cost x % equity)
			3.050%	Premium for small company
			1.099%	Premium for specific city risk, Santa Monica
Total, cost of capital			**9.837%**	

CALCULATION OF DEBT RATIOS

	Common Shares Outstanding Millions	Average Price Per Share 2011	Total Equity Millions-$	Total Debt Millions-$	Total Capital Millions-$	Debt/ Capital Ratio	Beta
BRE Properties	75.6	47.0	3,551.3	1,685.7	5,237.0	32.19%	1.05
Equity Residential	300.2	56.2	5,277.6	9,721.1	14,998.7	64.81%	1.10
Realty Income Corp.	133.4	33.1	4,408.4	2,055.2	6,463.6	31.80%	0.90
Washington REIT	66.3	30.0	1,988.1	1,184.2	3,172.3	37.33%	1.00
UDR Inc,	223.3	23.7	5,282.0	3,918.4	9,200.4	42.59%	1.05
Federal Realty	63.7	84.3	2,110.4	1,638.5	3,748.9	43.71%	1.10
Kimko Realty Corp.	406.9	16.9	6,877.2	4,114.4	10,991.6	37.43%	1.30
Average/Total	1269.4	$23.2	29,495.1	24,317.5	53,812.6	45.19%	1.07
Assumed Optimum						53.11%	

The optimum debt depends on specific circumstances. Higher debt is possible if the firm has minimum risk
The firms selected are actively traded in the public market, shown by listing in Value Line. The primary
investments for this group of companies is residential real estate, with some investments in mixed-use.
The data reflects financial results through 2011, with beta calculated on performance for 5 years, 2007-2011
Optimum debt as a percent of total capital is assumed higher than typical for the industry, for leverage.
The assumed optimum is calculated as: =((MAXA(E113:E119)+(AVERAGE(E113:E119)))/2)
This calculation assumes an optimum that is higher than group average, but lower than the group maximum
The average price per share is the average of high and low prices for 2011. Total capital is equity plus debt.
Equity is at market value, determined by recent market prices for the common shares, plus liabilities.
Equity value is defined as number of common shares times the market price, with no premium for control.

INCOME TAX RATES
Combined Tax Effects

Income before tax	$100.00
Income Tax, State	11.00
Income, after state tax	$89.00
Income Tax, Federal	31.15
Income after federal and state tax	$57.85

Tax Rates

State Tax Rate, %	11.00%
Federal Tax Rate, %	35.00%
Combined tax rate, %	42.15%

The combined rate reflect the deduction of state income tax for federal tax purposes. The 35% maximum
corporate rate applies to tax years beginning on or after Jan.1, 1993, 1993 Act 13221(a), 26 USC 11(b)(1).

FEDERAL RESERVE statistical release

H.15 (519) SELECTED INTEREST RATES

Yields in percent per annum

For use at 2:30 p.m. Eastern Time

June 22, 2015

Instruments	2015 Jun 15	2015 Jun 16	2015 Jun 17	2015 Jun 18	2015 Jun 19	Week Ending Jun 19	Week Ending Jun 12	2015 May
Federal funds (effective)[1][2][3]	0.13	0.14	0.14	0.14	0.13	0.13	0.13	0.12
Commercial Paper[3][4][5][6]								
Nonfinancial								
1-month	n.a.	0.09	n.a.	0.08	0.08	0.08	0.10	0.08
2-month	n.a.	0.07	0.15	0.08	n.a.	0.10	0.11	0.10
3-month	n.a.	0.10	0.19	0.13	n.a.	0.14	0.14	0.12
Financial								
1-month	0.10	0.11	0.11	0.11	0.12	0.11	0.11	0.09
2-month	0.16	0.15	0.15	0.15	0.16	0.15	0.14	0.12
3-month	0.17	0.20	0.21	0.19	0.20	0.19	0.18	0.15
Eurodollar deposits (London)[3][7]								
1-month	0.19	0.19	0.19	0.19	0.19	0.19	0.19	0.19
3-month	0.30	0.30	0.30	0.30	0.33	0.31	0.30	0.30
6-month	0.43	0.43	0.43	0.43	0.46	0.44	0.43	0.43
Bank prime loan[2][3][8]	3.25	3.25	3.25	3.25	3.25	3.25	3.25	3.25
Discount window primary credit[2][9]	0.75	0.75	0.75	0.75	0.75	0.75	0.75	0.75
U.S. government securities								
Treasury bills (secondary market)[3][4]								
4-week	0.00	0.00	0.00	-0.01	-0.01	-0.00	0.01	0.01
3-month	0.02	0.01	0.01	0.01	0.01	0.01	0.02	0.02
6-month	0.11	0.11	0.10	0.08	0.05	0.09	0.09	0.08
1-year	0.25	0.25	0.24	0.23	0.22	0.24	0.26	0.22
Treasury constant maturities								
Nominal[10]								
1-month	0.00	0.00	0.00	0.00	0.00	0.00	0.01	0.01
3-month	0.02	0.01	0.01	0.01	0.01	0.01	0.02	0.02
6-month	0.11	0.11	0.10	0.08	0.05	0.09	0.09	0.08
1-year	0.28	0.28	0.27	0.26	0.25	0.27	0.28	0.24
2-year	0.72	0.71	0.67	0.66	0.65	0.68	0.73	0.61
3-year	1.10	1.08	1.03	1.03	0.99	1.05	1.12	0.98
5-year	1.71	1.68	1.63	1.65	1.59	1.65	1.75	1.54
7-year	2.11	2.07	2.05	2.08	1.99	2.06	2.16	1.93
10-year	2.36	2.32	2.32	2.35	2.26	2.32	2.42	2.20
20-year	2.83	2.79	2.82	2.86	2.76	2.81	2.88	2.69
30-year	3.09	3.06	3.09	3.09	3.05	3.09	3.14	2.96
Inflation indexed[11]								
5-year	0.07	0.01	-0.06	-0.02	-0.04	-0.01	0.11	-0.10
7-year	0.37	0.31	0.29	0.32	0.28	0.31	0.44	0.27
10-year	0.51	0.44	0.42	0.46	0.40	0.45	0.57	0.33
20-year	0.89	0.82	0.84	0.89	0.81	0.85	0.95	0.70
30-year	1.12	1.05	1.09	1.14	1.07	1.09	1.18	0.96
Inflation-indexed long-term average[12]	0.88	0.82	0.85	0.88	0.81	0.85	0.94	0.74
Interest rate swaps[13]								
1-year	0.55	0.56	0.57	0.51	0.50	0.54	0.56	0.48
2-year	0.96	0.96	0.99	0.90	0.88	0.94	0.98	0.86
3-year	1.32	1.31	1.35	1.25	1.21	1.29	1.35	1.20
4-year	1.60	1.59	1.63	1.54	1.49	1.57	1.64	1.46
5-year	1.83	1.82	1.86	1.78	1.72	1.80	1.87	1.68
7-year	2.15	2.15	2.18	2.12	2.06	2.13	2.21	1.99
10-year	2.44	2.44	2.45	2.42	2.36	2.42	2.50	2.26
30-year	2.86	2.87	2.88	2.88	2.82	2.86	2.92	2.70
Corporate bonds								
Moody's seasoned								
Aaa[14]	4.19	4.15	4.15	4.22	4.14	4.17	4.20	3.98
Baa	5.09	5.06	5.08	5.17	5.08	5.10	5.13	4.89
State & local bonds[15]				3.79		3.79	3.87	3.76
Conventional mortgages[16]				4.00		4.00	4.04	3.84

See overleaf for footnotes.

n.a.   Not available.

7. Ethics

For major city, state and federal issues, important decisions necessarily involve ethical factors, not just analysis of the meaning of statutes and court decisions. The effect of the decisions on individual lives and on the entire economy must be considered. It is not sufficient to merely follow precedent or to assume that the future will be similar to the past. New technology and new generations lead to different circumstances.

Rapid Reporting of Facts

Today, we experience the new normal, based on a increasing use of the internet for purchases, selection of cities for vacations, and with special emphasis on the quality of lodging, including the proximity to the beach, high quality shopping, and major universities.

The new circumstances require a fresh assessment of the refined standards for ethical decisions and actions. For the selection of cities to visit, many tourists reply on personal reports from other people combined with travel books, published by Michelin, Fodor's, Lonely Planet, DK Eyewitness, and other sources. However, for selection of specific lodging and restaurants, the current focus is on reviews from other travelers, as reported on the internet. For Airbnb, prompt, detailed, insightful reviews on of the lodging experience allow travelers to select lodging based on the experience of other guests.

This rapid, two-way review process allows prompt corrective responses within the system, so that there is no need for city regulations, city enforcement, or city involvement of any kind. As stated by several responses to the Federal Trade Commission, the sharing economy and short term rentals are best left alone from government involvement. As with shown by the rapid and effective development of internet commerce, wherein taxes were intentionally minimized, the business firms effectively designed innovative and adaptive systems without inefficient government regulations and interference.

Based on recent personal observation and prompt internet communication, the older methods of deception and misrepresentation traditionally used by politicians and used car salesmen, are no longer effective, because of the speed and wide internet dispersal of reports regarding the facts and the nature of the deception.

Definitions

The following definitions are adopted for the purposes of clarity in discussion:

Ethics -- The study of right versus wrong decisions and actions.

Culture -- The way in which a society solves its problems.

Morality -- The fundamental standards of behavior for a society.

Law -- The formalized decision rules and procedures for resolving disputes.

Critical Issue -- A fundamental and controversial problem which must be resolved to attain an objective.

Ethics and morals were used as having identical meaning, in early usage, due to the etymological basis. The Greek word *ethos* and the Latin word *mores* both mean cultural habits or customs. In current usage, refers to reflective evaluation concerning conduct. In current usage, morals refers to habitual or customary actions and standards of conduct accepted by the society.

The early Greek and Latin derivation is reflected in the definition found in Black's Law Dictionary:

... moral action, conduct, motive or character ... moral feelings, duties or conduct .... professionally right or befitting; conforming to professional standards of conduct. *Black's Law Dictionary*, Fifth Edition, p. 496, citing *Kraushaar v. La Vin*, 181 Misc 508, 42 N.Y.S.2d 857, 859.

Ethics is concerned with right and wrong actions. Ethics is moral philosophy, which includes two major approaches (1) the analytical study of the meaning and nature of moral concepts and moral actions and (2) development of authentic normative standards and criteria for justifying rules and judgments of what is right and wrong, good and bad. *Encyclopedia Brittanica*, Vol.6, 1977, p. 977.

Examples of Ethical Issues

The following are examples of from actual events. These types of circumstances typically arise from the desire for high short range profits, but the long range result is litigation, unfavorable publicity, loss of clientele, changed statutes, and ultimate long range financial failure.

Non-Disclosure. A major corporation failed to disclose the contingent liabilities that could result from unfavorable financial performance for unconsolidated subsidiaries, joint ventures and partnerships. The existence of subsidiaries was disclosed, but only in a footnote. The firm made no disclosure of subsidiary losses or the market value of subsidiary equity. Generally Accepted Accounting Procedures (GAAP) allow subsidiaries to be shown on the balance sheet as an investment at cost, as contrasted to current market value. Similarly, contingent liabilities such as environmental cleanup obligations or pending litigation can be mentioned in a footnote. However, under SEC Rule 10b-5, a public corporation is required to disclose information that is required to protect investor interests. Fraud does not require material misrepresentation; fraud also results from non-disclosure when there is an obligation to disclose.

Fiduciary Breach. A major pension plan declined to honor vested health benefits on employee retirement. Due to failure to keep adequate records, the pension plan informed the employee on retirement that he had no vested health benefits, with the result that the employee filed a late claim for the health benefits. Rejection was based on state law that requires the employee to claim health benefits within 120 days after leaving employment. However, as a fiduciary, the pension plan is required to correct their errors.

Deceit. A major defense contractor failed to disclose incipient failure of the flight control system and the critical electronic countermeasures (ECM) equipment. The employee who documented the issues was terminated. After litigation, the company paid over $30 million to the government to settle criminal fraud charges, then the largest fine in corporate history, plus $825,000 to the terminated employee. For the next decade, the government selected other companies in major design competitions.

False Billing. A well-known attorney won a major award for a client under a contingent fee agreement which was silent regarding litigation costs, but which gave 40 percent of the proceeds to the attorney. However, the attorney kept 90 percent of the proceeds, based on charging paralegal fees and word processing costs, and costs for four other clients. State rules prevent cost sharing amount clients without informed written client consent. Ordinarily, paralegal fees and word processing costs are not client costs for contingent fee agreements. An attorney is a fiduciary for the client. After malpractice litigation including appeal, the attorney was found to be negligent and was required to pay $125,000 to the client.

Burdensome Litigation. A federal lawyer failed to stipulate to facts which should not be reasonably in dispute, arguing that his actions increase revenue to the government due to the high cost of litigation.

Employees are required to avoid any action which might create the appearance of impeding government efficiency or economy or affecting adversely the confidence of the public in the integrity of the government. *Executive Order* 11222 as amended by *Executive Order* 11590.

Both parties are required to stipulate to all issues, facts and application of law to the facts that are not reasonably in dispute, *U.S. Tax Court Rules of Practice and Procedure*, Rule 91(f). A lawyer should avoid even the appearance of professional impropriety, Canon 9, *Model Code of Professional Responsibility*, American Bar Association, p. 47.

Lack of Diligence. The real-life agent 007, following many years of active service for British Intelligence in the Middle-East, was found dead in his car in the Barrego Springs area north of San Diego. His family was found murdered. Surprisingly, local authorities deemed the death a murder/suicide. British authorities disagreed with the finding. Private investigation revealed multiple unexplained "accidental" deaths in the area, combined with inconsistencies in the reported facts.

The FBI and the State Attorney General declined to intervene. Federal court civil litigation, supported by relatives of the deceased, introduced evidence that contradicted the findings of the local authorities. However, the federal judge failed to review the case with patience and diligence. The case was appealed to the Ninth Circuit, but was settled out of court to minimize plaintiff costs.

> A Judge should perform the duties of his office impartially and diligently...A judge should accord to every person ...full right to be heard according to law, Canon 3, Code of Judicial Conduct, *Model Code of Professional Responsibility*, ABA, p.62.

For each of the above cases, there are evident violations of explicit standards of behavior. However, the actions have the color of justification on the basis of personal advancement, maximization of profit, and efficiency. For many circumstances, the justification is false. Instead, correct decisions and correct actions are required. The standard is measured by the effect on other people, including the client, the suppliers, the customers, and the general public. For ethical decisions, the decision criteria cannot be the effect on short-term corporate profit or executive compensation.

City Misrepresentation. It is obvious that city councils may not assert that a tail is a leg, and proclaim that all dogs in the city are now taxed on the basis of five legs. However, as hubris, many cities are now asserting that a home is a *de facto* hotel, if the home is rented for less than 30 days. Clearly, such mischaracterization is fraud, as an intentional inaccurate description of the actual situation.

The public relies on judges, attorneys, and city officials to uphold both the state constitution and the U.S. Constitution. However, in the case of the Transient Occupancy Tax, many cities simply adopt the new local tax <u>without a vote</u> of the public, although the California Constitution Article XIIIC clearly states that any new local tax <u>requires a vote</u> of the public. The deception is to <u>shift the meaning</u> of the term hotel so that a home suddenly becomes a hotel. Clearly, this behavior by a city council is in the worst traditions of political behavior, and is a violation of both relevant law and ethics.

The Decision Criteria

A correct decision requires realistic review of each alternative course of action, and selection from the options based on a decision criteria. The objective, which results in the decision criteria, is the most important element. For most situations, critical issues involve facts and circumstances that are unclear, ambiguous, and controversial, so that even experts may disagree as to the correct decision. To assure the optimum decision, the decision criteria must reflect <u>sound ethical values</u>.

The foundation of the decision criteria is the social values that are accepted as correct, which are based on the *highest ideals* shared by the profession, the industry, the nation, and the world. Over thousands of years, separate cultures have derived remarkably similar basic standards of behavior. These basic values have been refined over thousands of years of interaction, conflict resolution, and inquiry. Accordingly, the principles of ethical behavior form a solid foundation for correct decisions and actions.

The basic principles of ethics require <u>intelligent caring for others</u>, as contrasted to self. The basic idea is vicarious understanding of the needs of others, and full dedication to serving these needs.

Correct strategy, based on ethics, is important. The basic strategy is <u>continuous improvement</u> in quality and performance, designed to serve customer needs. Contrary to ideas advanced by some theorists, maximum revenue or maximum profit is <u>not </u>the ultimate goal. Instead, <u>service of customer needs</u> is the goal. Then, the satisfied customer will produce company wealth. Price competition may lead to insufficient profit to stay in business. As a correct strategy, price competition is avoided through emphasis on <u>quality</u>, distinctive products, and customer satisfaction. People will pay for quality. Instead of seeking to maximize tax revenue, each city should focus on efficiency, improved service to all citizens in the domain, and review each issue on a cost vs. benefit analysis.

The Results of Greed

Based on hubris, it is common for a city council member to ignore facts, and to focus on personal goals, as shown by a standard policy of "...don't bother me with the facts, my mind is made up". For some proposed city ordinances, especially when the process involved questionable contributions for reelection, side benefits to the city council members, or a seemingly irrational weight to union preferences or to focus on impractical objectives, it becomes obvious that the litigation risks far exceed any benefit from the improper ordinance. Improper review of facts or attempts to distort the results by preventing information from being heard leads to questions of procedural due process, especially when the city hearings intentionally exclude or prevent opposing viewpoints but give exaggerated exposure to supporting views.

It should be obvious that unethical decisions and wrongful acts whether for defective design and manufacturing, or professional malpractice, or false claims on federal contracts, demonstrate that greed leads to ruin. Clearly, ethics determines the selection of objection, the scope of the alternatives reviewed, the nature of the decision criteria, the risk tolerance, and extent of disclosure.

For many complex decisions, there is a growing trend to rely on calculations based on mathematical models, which allow a change of conditions to determine which factors are sensitive. The basic ethical problem is disclosure of the source and accuracy of the input data, and the conditions and alternatives that were considered. A detailed calculation can give the impression of correctness, even if the underlying assumptions are unreasonable, unrealistic, and not based on measurements. Calculation assumptions must be reasonable, symbols must be defined to allow effective communications and full understanding, and critical assumptions must be tested against a range of possibilities to determine the effect of the assumption. Sensitive issues must be disclosed and described, to allow seasoned judgment based on relevant information.

For many cases, the results of the calculation are misinterpreted, due to lack of understanding regarding the assumptions, the undisclosed issues, and the sensitivity of the result to the assumptions. Accordingly, it is essential to describe the implications of the calculation details, including unpalatable results.

Decisions and Actions

Ethical issues arise with regard to both decisions and actions. Primary emphasis must be on the decision, because actions result from decisions. In ethics, as in criminal law, there are two major elements:

mens rea -- wrongful purpose; willful intent to do an improper act

actus reus -- the wrongful physical act

The decision to act implies a period of detached reflection and thoughtful deliberation of the consequences of the act. For matters with potentially serious impacts and implications, substantial analysis and review of benefits versus costs is required. The deliberative process should include sufficient time to review the critical issues, discern the alternative courses of action and make a selection based on a decision criteria. The decision criteria is typically based on inherent ethical values.

Justification of Actions

For many actions that involve ethical issues, it is common for the decision maker to adopt a socially acceptable goal to justify predatory practices. The initial goal is later distorted to justify wrongful acts.

Initial Goals

Satisfy customer needs

Achieve growth in earnings and profits

Distorted Goals

Increase reported quarterly earnings

Maximize the personal wealth of the executive

In many cases, unethical actions are in the penumbra of the law, in the grey area not prohibited by the law, but on the edge of prohibited conduct. However, the individual typically makes an intentional assessment and decision that the issues and facts can be obscured to lower the risk of unfavorable consequences. The typical strategy is to report the actual facts in a inaccurate, incomplete or distorted manner, and to prevent or obstruct observation or audit of the actual situation. The strategy of deception includes failure to disclose, misleading innuendo, ambiguity, and lack of particularity. Deception is the hallmark of unethical actions. Badges of fraud include document destruction, misleading nomenclature, failure to disclose, internal inconsistency, and lack of consistency with external reality.

The deceptive justification is intended to camouflage the actual intent. The physical act can be observed; the wrongful purpose must be inferred from the act and the circumstances.

> Intent is the design, resolve or determination with which a person acts, *Witters v. U.S.*, 106 F.2d 837, 840. Intent is a state of mind that is rarely susceptible to direct proof, but must ordinarily be inferred from observable facts, *Reinhard v. Lawrence*, 41 Cal. App.2d 741. Intent denotes that the actor desires to cause consequences of his act or that he believes that the consequences are substantially certain to result, *Restatement of Torts*, 2d, Sec. 8A. Motive is the underlying cause that prompts a person to act or fail to act; intent is the state of mind with which the act is done or omitted, *Black's Law Dictionary*, p. 727.

Causes of Unethical Actions

Changes in Culture and Values. Obligations and requirements result from human interaction. The social relationships and culture results in standards of expected behavior. The behavioral standards exhibit increased formality and more precise definition with increased severity of impact on society, ranging from etiquette to criminal statutes and international treaties. The tax statutes are extremely complex. The congressional intent is mixed, including intent to provide investment incentives to stimulate the national economy combined with the intent to imposes taxes fairly.

Mass Media as a Source of Values. Over a period of many centuries, society values were transmitted through carefully controlled means. In recent years, television and motion pictures have emphasized self-interest and materialistic values. Mass media values are in sharp contrast to the former values of hard work, the value of private property, consideration for the feelings of other people and the importance of wisdom. Values promoted by the mass media include conspicuous consumption, leisure, and reliance on emotion instead of intellect.

Influence of Formal Organizations. The lives of many persons are spent as part of large formal organizations, with levels of authority and limits on individual initiative. The result is less reliance on the importance of individual decisions and actions. The individual may feel inadequate to influence organization actions. Executive leadership may be made ineffective due to group resistance to change and middle management baronies.

Role Models and the Power Elite. In prior years, human dignity and integrity was of primary importance. Persons with high moral standards were regarded as heroic. Today, the power elite are persons with high income and positions of authority, even if the source of wealth or power was based on questionable ethical actions. Statesmen have been replaced by politicians funded by Political Action Committees. Nobel prize winners are overshadowed by sports figures and rock musicians. Accordingly, individual behavior can be expected to conform to the standard established by the relevant role model.

Critical Issues

Balance. The ethical decision must *balance* benefits versus unsought consequences, long run versus short run effects, and personal benefit versus social impacts. Without balance, a specific value may receive disproportionate emphasis, resulting in distortion and wrongful actions.

Mature Personal Judgment. Ethical actions result from refined and mature individual mental adjustment. The characteristics of psychological maturity have been defined:

> (1) Ability to appraise reality with reasonable accuracy, with consideration for surface and deeper motivations and without distortion due to wishes, fears or emotions.

(2) Ability to love others, identified by willingness to do what is best for the loved one even if the action involves substantial personal inconvenience or is temporarily provocative of self displeasure.

(3) Capacity to work productively, due to realistic benefits that accrue to self and others.

(4) Possession of an effective conscience, with preventative impact to avoid behavior which would be destructive to self or others.

(5) Ability to find gratification for basic needs, including delay of immediate gratification for long-range achievement and which entail a minimum of suffering for self and others. Charles K. Hofling, *Textbook of Psychiatry for Medical Practice*, Third edition, Philadelphia: J. B. Lipencott, 1975, pp.33-35.

Legal Standards

The federal government has established specific minimum standards of conduct by law. The standards are applicable to firms, private citizens and government employees. Prohibited acts are clearly described. The following are typical standards imposed by federal law:

False statements. Knowing and willful concealment, cover up of a material fact, or statements or representations that are false, fictitious or fraudulent. 18 USC §1001.

False claim. Making of a false, fictitious or fraudulent claim for payment by federal government, or a conspiracy to obtain payment or allowance of any false claim. 18 USC §286 and §287.

Civil damages are specified for making or using a false record or statement to make a claim against the government or conceal, avoid or decrease an obligation to pay money to the government. Knowingly is defined as having actual knowledge, acting in deliberate ignorance or with reckless disregard of the truth or falsity of the information. No proof of specific intent is required. 31 USC §3729, as modified by P.L. 99-562, Oct.27, 1986.

An individual may bring a civil action on behalf of the government for violation of 31 USC 3729. If the government proceeds with the action, the private party *qui tam* plaintiff shall receive up to 25 percent of the proceeds of the action or settlement. An employee who is discharged, demoted, suspended, threatened, harassed or discriminated against by the employer because of lawful acts by the in furtherance of this action shall be entitled to all relief necessary to make the employee whole. 31 USC 3730, P.L. 99-562, Oct.27, 1986.

False credit statement. Knowing false statement, or willful overvaluation of property, to influence the action of a federally insured banking institution. 18 USC §1014.

Mail fraud. Use of the mails to defraud or to obtain money or property through false or fraudulent pretenses, representations or promises. 18 USC §1341.

Obstruction of proceedings. Endeavor to influence, intimidate or impede any witness or obstruct or impede the due and proper administration of the law, in any proceeding pending before any department or agency of the United States. 18 USC §1505.

Obstruction of criminal investigations. Endeavor to obstruct, delay or prevent the communication of information relating to a federal crime, by means of bribery, misrepresentation, intimidation, treats of force, use of force, or injury to a person or property. 18 USC §1510.

Investment of funds from illegal activities. Use or invest any proceeds from illegal activities in any firm which is engaged in interstate commerce. The Racketeer Influenced and Corrupt Organizations (RICO) Act, 18 USC §1962.

Tax fraud. Willful attempt to evade or defeat any tax, 26 USC §7201. Willful failure to pay any tax, make a return, keep any records or supply any information. 26 USC §7203. Willful delivery or disclosure of any document known to be false as to any material matter, 26 USC §7207.

Note that there is a clear distinction between (1) minimization of taxes and (2) fraud. "Any attempt to reduce avoid, minimize or alleviate taxes by legitimate means is permissible... One who *avoids* tax does not conceal or misrepresent. He shapes events to reduce or eliminate tax liability ... *Evasion* on the other hand involves deceit, subterfuge, camouflage, concealment, some attempt to color or obscure events, or making things seem other than they are ..." *IRS Handbook for Special Agents*, Section 312.

Bribery. Directly or indirectly, asks, demands, exacts, solicits, seeks, accepts, receives or agrees to receive *anything of value* for himself or any other person or entity in return for being influenced in his performance of any official act. 18 USC §201(c),(g).

Embezzlement and theft. Embezzle or wrongfully convert to personal use the money or property of another, 18 USC §654. Convert to any other purpose or use property solicited for the use of the federal government, 18 USC §663.

Federal Ethical Standards

Federal employees are required to observe federal ethical standards, clearly stated an executive order:

> no employee shall *solicit or accept*, directly or indirectly, any gift, gratuity, favor, entertainment, loan or any other *thing of monetary value* ... from any person, corporation or group, which ... has ... financial relationships with his agency ... conducts operations or activities which are regulated by his agency or ... has interests which may be substantially affected by the performance or nonperformance of his official duty ....
>
> It is the intent of this section that employees avoid any action, whether or not specifically prohibited ...which might result in, or create the appearance of
>
> (1) using public office for private gain;

(2) giving preferential treatment to any organization or person;

(3) impeding government efficiency or economy;

(4) making a government decision outside official channels;

(5) affecting adversely the confidence of the public in the integrity of the government.

Executive Order No. 11222, *Standards of Ethical Conduct for Government Officers and Employees*, May 8, 1965, as amended by Executive Order No. 11590, April 23, 1971. (emphasis added). Documented as a note to 18 USC 201.

An employee shall avoid any action ... which might result in or create the appearance of using public office for private gain, giving preferential treatment to any person, impeding Government efficiency or economy, losing complete independence or impartiality, making a Government decision outside of official channels or affecting adversely the confidence of the public in the integrity of the Government. 5 CFR 735.201a.

Ethical Leadership

Many ethical problems involve wrongful acts by subordinates. The following approaches are suggested for improvement in organization conduct:

Selective staffing -- emphasize moral standards in the selection of executives and managers

Emphasis on performance-- emphasize the high ground with standards for excellence and quality

Moral leadership -- the executive must provide an example of high ethical principles through actions.

Suggested Decision Criteria

The following criteria are suggested for ethical decisions:

1. **Truth.** Truth is defined as an accurate description of reality. Reality is defined as that which exists apart from the cognitive process of the individual. Deception, misleading representations, and failure to disclose are the badges of unethical action.

2. **Vicarious impact**. The correctness of the action must be judged from the viewpoint of the *injured party*.

3. **Sensitivity to others.** Even the *feelings* of others must be protected. Mere protection of property rights is insufficient. Benefits to self will result from emphasis on the interests of others.

4. **Non-Materialism**. Emphasis must be placed on long-term intangible benefits, such as increase in wisdom. Greed is not a virtue. Increase in personal or corporate wealth is not an acceptable justification for actions.

5. **Social responsibility**. Ethical standards are higher than legal obligations. Mere compliance with legal standards is inadequate. Individuals and firms have an ethical obligation to serve needs, solve problems, and improve the quality of life for other persons.

6. **Long range impact.** Personal wealth results from personal relationships based on trust and confidence. This trust and personal confidence is the result of ethical actions over many years. Short run benefits typically backfire and result in ruin.

7. **Superior effort**. Diligence is required. High quality performance and continuous improvement is essential.

Time and effort is required for correct, ethical decisions. Emphasis must be placed on the selection of goals that offer benefits to other persons, not just to the decision maker. In the short run, there may be substantial unsought consequences for the decision maker. In the long run, the benefits from ethical decisions are substantially certain to result in success.

Exhibit A

Economic Factors

House Prices, Inflation, Mortgage Rates, Yield Premium

Monthly House Price Index for U.S.

Purchase-Only, Seasonally Adjusted Index, January 1991 - Present

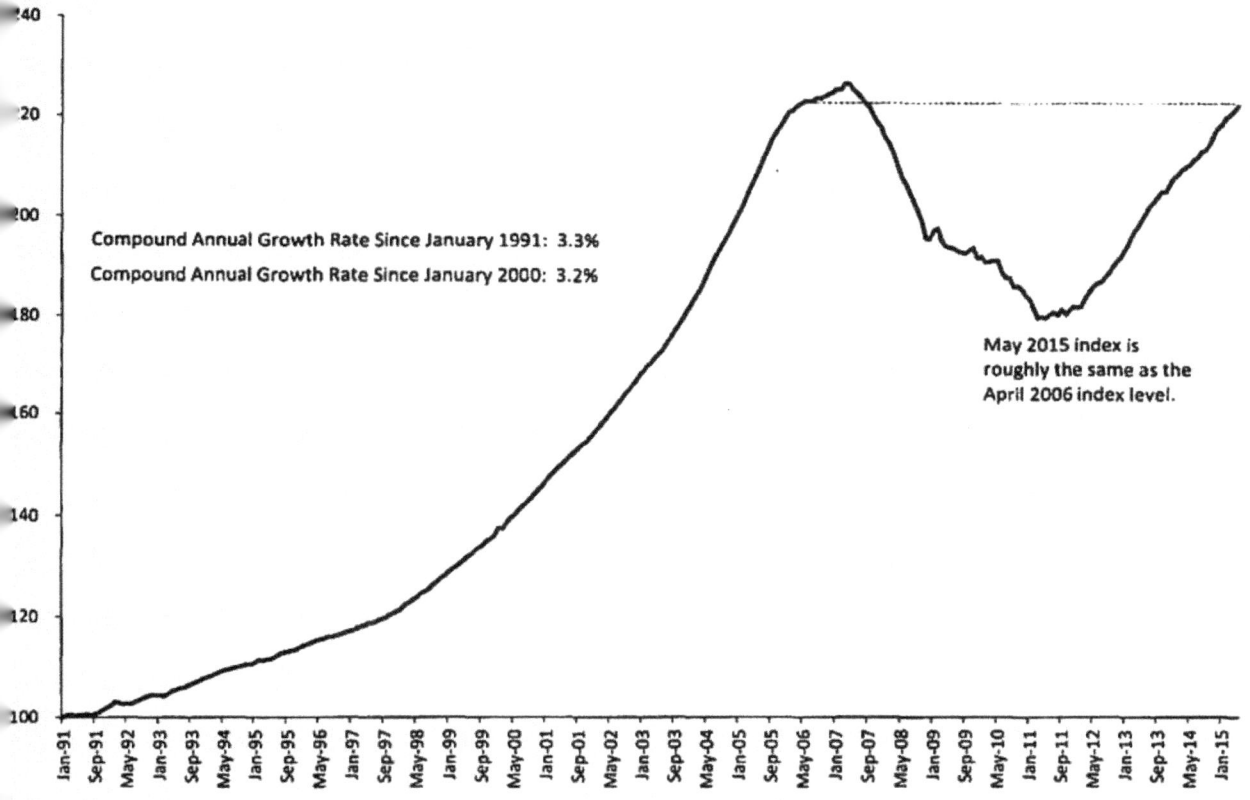

Compound Annual Growth Rate Since January 1991: 3.3%

Compound Annual Growth Rate Since January 2000: 3.2%

May 2015 index is roughly the same as the April 2006 index level.

Source: FHFA

Consumer Price Index-Urban (CPI-U), U.S. City Average, 1913-2015
Cumulative

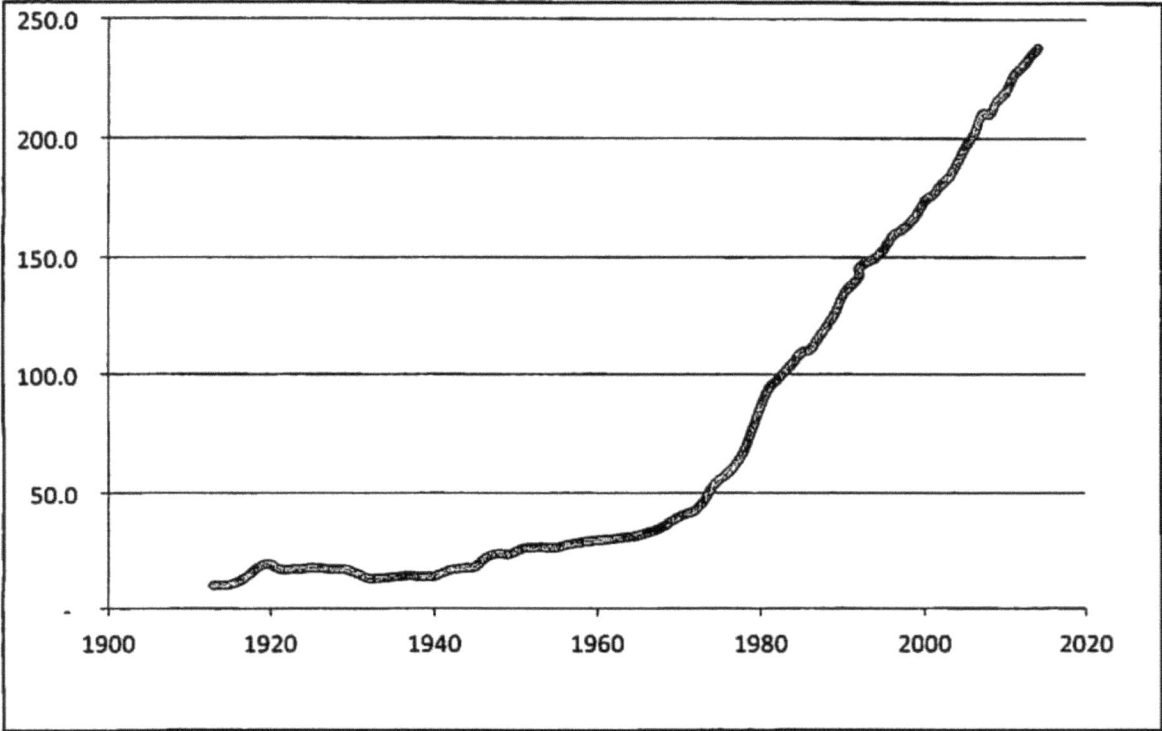

Consumer Price Index-Urban (CPI-U), U.S. City Average, 1913-2015
Percent Annual Increase

ation,%

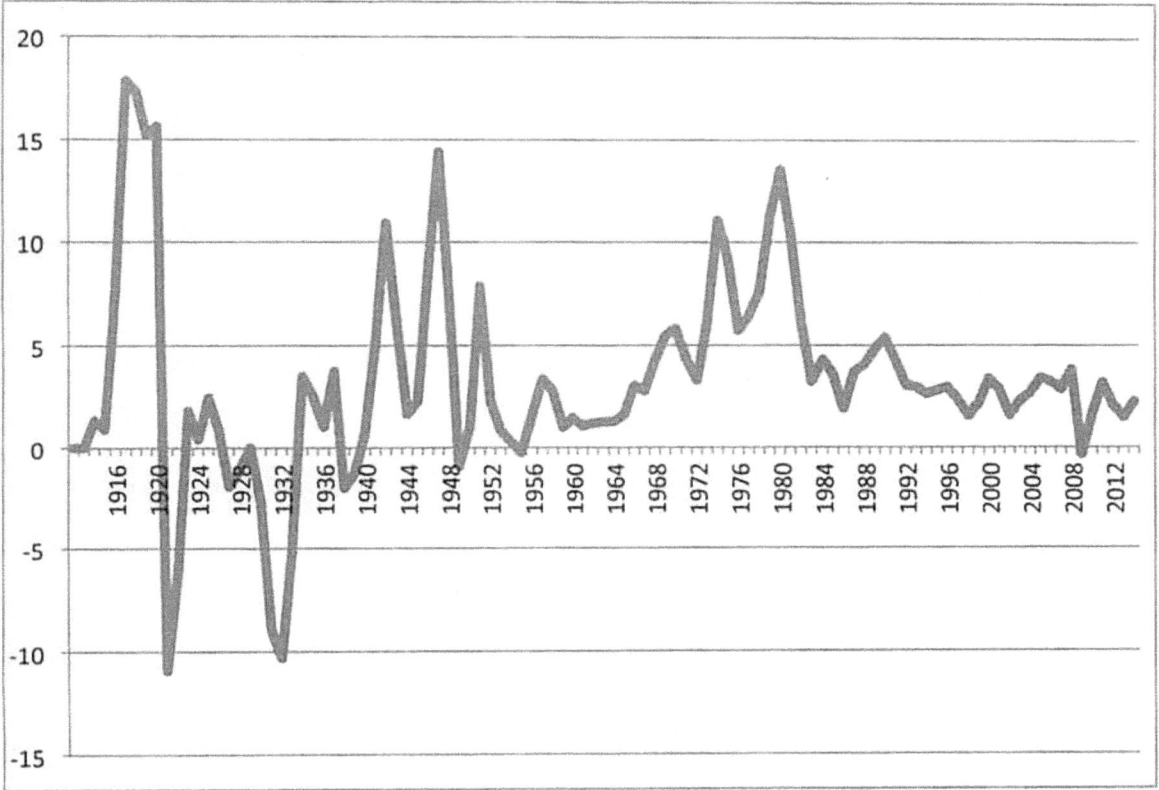

Consumer Price Index-Urban (CPI-U), U.S. City Average, 1913-2015
Inflation, % per year
Data is not seasonally adjusted

Year	Jan.	Feb.	Mar.	Apr.	May	June	July	Aug.	Sep.	Oct.	Nov.	Dec.	Dec to Dec	Annual Average
1970	37.8	38.0	38.2	38.5	38.6	38.8	39.0	39.0	39.2	39.4	39.6	39.8	5.57	5.84
1971	39.8	39.9	40.0	40.1	40.3	40.6	40.7	40.8	40.8	40.9	40.9	41.1	3.27	4.29
1972	41.1	41.3	41.4	41.5	41.6	41.7	41.9	42.0	42.1	42.3	42.4	42.5	3.41	3.27
1973	42.6	42.9	43.3	43.6	43.9	44.2	44.3	45.1	45.2	45.6	45.9	46.2	8.71	6.18
1974	46.6	47.2	47.8	48.0	48.6	49.0	49.4	50.0	50.6	51.1	51.5	51.9	12.34	11.05
1975	52.1	52.5	52.7	52.9	53.2	53.6	54.2	54.3	54.6	54.9	55.3	55.5	6.94	9.14
1976	55.6	55.8	55.9	56.1	56.5	56.8	57.1	57.4	57.6	57.9	58.0	58.2	4.86	5.74
1977	58.5	59.1	59.5	60.0	60.3	60.7	61.0	61.2	61.4	61.6	61.9	62.1	6.70	6.50
1978	62.5	62.9	63.4	63.9	64.5	65.2	65.7	66.0	66.5	67.1	67.4	67.7	9.02	7.63
1979	68.3	69.1	69.8	70.6	71.5	72.3	73.1	73.8	74.6	75.2	75.9	76.7	13.29	11.25
1980	77.8	78.9	80.1	81.0	81.8	82.7	82.7	83.3	84.0	84.8	85.5	86.3	12.52	13.55
1981	87.0	87.9	88.5	89.1	89.8	90.6	91.6	92.3	93.2	93.4	93.7	94.0	8.92	10.33
1982	94.3	94.6	94.5	94.9	95.8	97.0	97.5	97.7	97.9	98.2	98.0	97.6	3.83	6.13
1983	97.8	97.9	97.9	98.6	99.2	99.5	99.9	100.2	100.7	101.0	101.2	101.3	3.79	3.21
1984	101.9	102.4	102.6	103.1	103.4	103.7	104.1	104.5	105.0	105.3	105.3	105.3	3.95	4.30
1985	105.5	106.0	106.4	106.9	107.3	107.6	107.8	108.0	108.3	108.7	109.0	109.3	3.80	3.55
1986	109.6	109.3	108.8	108.6	108.9	109.5	109.5	109.7	110.2	110.3	110.4	110.5	1.10	1.90
1987	111.2	111.6	112.1	112.7	113.1	113.5	113.8	114.4	115.0	115.3	115.4	115.4	4.43	3.66
1988	115.7	116.0	116.5	117.1	117.5	118.0	118.5	119.0	119.8	120.2	120.3	120.5	4.42	4.08
1989	121.1	121.6	122.3	123.1	123.8	124.1	124.4	124.6	125.0	125.6	125.9	126.1	4.65	4.83
1990	127.4	128.0	128.7	128.9	129.2	129.9	130.4	131.6	132.7	133.5	133.8	133.8	6.11	5.40
1991	134.6	134.8	135.0	135.2	135.6	136.0	136.2	136.6	137.2	137.4	137.8	137.9	3.06	4.23
1992	138.1	138.6	139.3	139.5	139.7	140.2	140.5	140.9	141.3	141.8	142.0	141.9	2.90	3.03
1993	142.6	143.1	143.6	144.0	144.2	144.4	144.4	144.8	145.1	145.7	145.8	145.8	2.75	2.95
1994	146.2	146.7	147.2	147.4	147.5	148.0	148.4	149.0	149.4	149.5	149.7	149.7	2.67	2.61
1995	150.3	150.9	151.4	151.9	152.2	152.5	152.5	152.9	153.2	153.7	153.6	153.5	2.54	2.81
1996	154.4	154.9	155.7	156.3	156.6	156.7	157.0	157.3	157.8	158.3	158.6	158.6	3.32	2.93
1997	159.1	159.6	160.0	160.2	160.1	160.3	160.5	160.8	161.2	161.6	161.5	161.3	1.70	2.34
1998	161.6	161.9	162.2	162.5	162.8	163.0	163.2	163.4	163.6	164.0	164.0	163.9	1.61	1.55
1999	164.3	164.5	165.0	166.2	166.2	166.2	166.7	167.1	167.9	168.2	168.3	168.3	2.68	2.19
2000	168.8	169.8	171.2	171.3	171.5	172.4	172.8	172.8	173.7	174.0	174.1	174.0	3.39	3.38
2001	175.1	175.8	176.2	176.9	177.7	178.0	177.5	177.5	178.3	177.7	177.4	176.7	1.55	2.83
2002	177.1	177.8	178.8	179.8	179.8	179.9	180.1	180.7	181.0	181.3	181.3	180.9	2.38	1.59
2003	181.7	183.1	184.2	183.8	183.5	183.7	183.9	184.6	185.2	185.0	184.5	184.3	1.88	2.27
2004	185.2	186.2	187.4	188.0	189.1	189.7	189.4	189.5	189.9	190.9	191.0	190.3	3.26	2.68
2005	190.7	191.8	193.3	194.6	194.4	194.5	195.4	196.4	198.8	199.2	197.6	196.8	3.4	3.39
2006	198.3	198.7	199.8	201.5	202.5	202.9	203.5	203.9	202.9	201.8	201.5	201.8	2.5	3.23
2007	202.4	203.5	205.4	206.7	207.9	208.4	208.3	207.9	208.5	208.9	210.2	210.0	4.1	2.85
2008	211.1	211.7	213.5	214.8	216.6	218.8	220.0	219.1	218.8	216.6	212.4	210.2	0.1	3.84
2009	211.1	212.2	212.7	213.2	213.9	215.7	215.4	215.8	216.0	216.2	216.3	215.9	2.7	(0.36)
2010	216.7	216.7	217.6	218.0	218.2	218.0	218.0	218.3	218.4	218.7	218.8	219.2	1.5	1.64
2011	220.2	221.3	223.5	224.9	226.0	225.7	225.9	226.5	226.9	226.4	226.2	226.2	3.2	3.18
2012	226.7	227.7	229.4	230.1	229.8	229.5	229.1	230.4	231.4	231.3	230.2	229.6	1.5	2.05
2013	230.3	232.2	232.8	232.5	232.9	233.5	233.6	233.9	234.1	233.5	233.1	234.0	1.9	1.50
2014	233.9	234.7	236.9	237.1	237.9	238.3	238.3	237.9	238.0	237.4	236.2	234.8	0.4	2.26
2015	233.7	234.7	236..11	236.6	237.8	238.6	238.7							

http://www.gpo.gov/fdsys/pkg/ECONI-2015-07/pdf/ECONI-2015-08-Pg23.pdf

Consumer Prices—All Urban Consumers

In July, the consumer price index for all urban consumers rose 0.1 percent; it was unchanged before seasonal adjustment. The index rose 0.2 percent from its year earlier level.

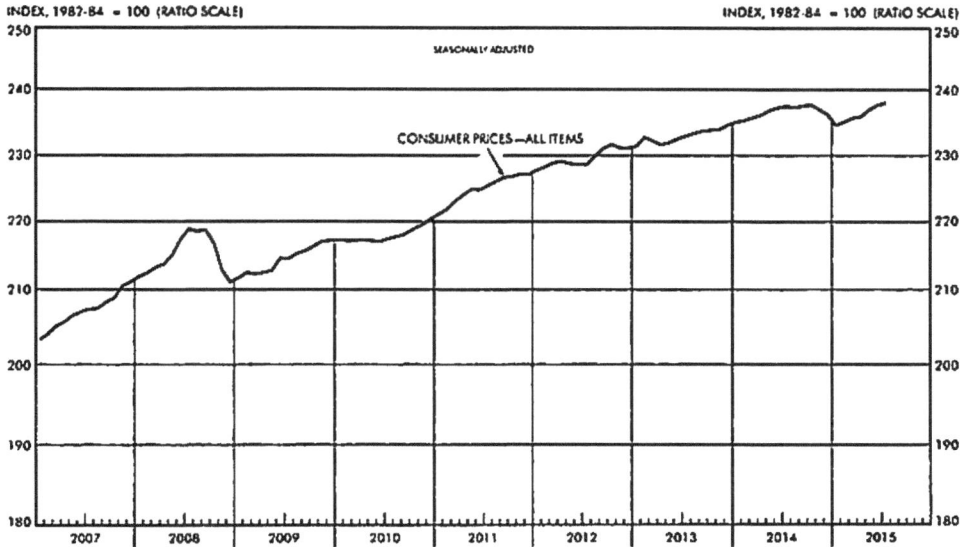

INDEX, 1982-84 = 100 (RATIO SCALE) — INDEX, 1982-84 = 100 (RATIO SCALE)

SOURCE: DEPARTMENT OF LABOR — COUNCIL OF ECONOMIC ADVISERS

[1982–84=100, except as noted, monthly data seasonally adjusted, except as noted by NSA]

Period	All items		All items less food and energy					Food			Energy		C-CPI-U (NSA)[3]
	Not seasonally adjusted (NSA)	Seasonally adjusted	Total[1]	Shelter	Medical care[2]	Apparel	New vehicles	Total[1]	At home	Away from home	Total[1,2]	Gasoline	
Rel. imp.[4]	100.0		77.613	32.759	7.705	3.317	3.525	14.056	8.256	5.810	8.313	4.199	
2005	195.3		200.9	224.4	323.2	119.5	137.9	190.7	189.8	193.4	177.1	194.7	113.7
2006	201.6		205.9	232.1	336.2	119.5	137.6	195.2	193.1	199.4	196.9	219.9	117.0
2007	207.342		210.729	240.611	351.054	118.998	136.254	202.916	201.245	206.659	207.723	237.959	119.957
2008	215.300		215.572	248.666	364.065	118.907	134.134	214.106	214.125	215.769	236.666	277.457	124.433
2009	214.537		219.235	249.354	375.613	120.078	135.623	217.955	215.124	223.272	193.126	201.565	123.850
2010	218.056		221.337	248.396	388.436	119.503	138.005	219.625	215.836	226.114	211.443	238.594	125.615
2011	224.939		225.008	251.646	400.258	122.111	141.883	227.842	226.201	231.401	243.909	301.694	129.453
2012	229.594		229.755	257.083	414.324	126.265	144.232	233.777	231.774	237.966	246.080	311.470	131.976
2013	232.957		233.806	263.056	425.134	127.411	145.783	237.037	233.969	243.068	244.409	302.577	....
2014	236.736		237.897	270.513	435.292	127.514	146.275	242.725	239.456	248.931	243.583	290.889	....
2014 July	238.250	237.596	238.217	270.869	435.903	128.259	146.311	243.165	240.039	249.210	249.755	303.044	136.424
Aug	237.852	237.409	238.340	271.489	436.047	127.751	146.511	243.843	240.777	249.601	245.512	294.814	136.162
Sept	238.031	237.626	238.686	272.166	436.872	127.907	146.554	244.654	241.619	250.570	243.843	292.119	136.248
Oct	237.433	237.751	239.120	272.833	437.608	127.567	146.752	245.125	242.053	251.100	240.883	286.208	135.962
Nov	236.151	237.067	239.304	273.501	439.419	126.706	146.770	245.632	242.309	251.387	230.897	265.500	135.033
Dec	234.812	236.284	239.445	274.016	441.370	125.643	146.656	246.237	242.893	252.628	220.070	240.998	134.113
2015 Jan	233.707	234.677	239.871	274.759	441.352	125.965	146.453	246.132	242.446	253.037	198.727	195.936	133.185
Feb	234.722	235.188	240.247	275.431	441.385	126.338	146.735	246.512	242.626	253.719	200.622	200.957	133.838
Mar	236.119	235.740	240.793	275.183	442.775	126.936	147.046	246.003	241.519	254.108	202.910	208.324	134.773
Apr	236.599	235.982	241.409	276.925	445.500	126.563	147.236	245.993	241.100	254.727	200.372	204.717	135.038
May	237.805	237.031	241.760	277.468	446.781	125.924	147.505	246.014	240.730	255.322	203.039	225.935	135.826
June	238.638	237.788	242.193	278.316	448.051	125.776	147.687	246.734	241.564	255.848	212.668	233.504	136.307
July	239.654	238.099	242.513	279.305	448.649	126.151	147.381	247.143	242.237	255.905	212.790	235.596	136.257

[1] Includes other items not shown separately.
[2] Commodities and services.
[3] Chained consumer price index (C-CPI-U) reflects the effect of substitution that consumers make across item categories in response to changes in relative prices.
[4] Relative importance, June 2015

Source: Department of Labor (Bureau of Labor Statistics)

23

http://www.gpo.gov/fdsys/pkg/ECONI-2015-08/pdf/ECONI-2015-08-Pg23.pdf

Interest Rate and Points On 30-Year Fixed-Rate Mortgages

	2015 Rate	2015 Pts	2014 Rate	2014 Pts	2013 Rate	2013 Pts	2012 Rate	2012 Pts	2011 Rate	2011 Pts
January	3.67	0.6	4.43	0.7	3.41	0.7	3.92	0.8	4.76	0.8
February	3.71	0.6	4.30	0.7	3.53	0.8	3.89	0.8	4.95	0.7
March	3.77	0.6	4.34	0.6	3.57	0.8	3.95	0.8	4.84	0.7
April	3.67	0.6	4.34	0.7	3.45	0.8	3.91	0.7	4.84	0.7
May	3.84	0.6	4.19	0.6	3.54	0.7	3.80	0.8	4.64	0.7
June	3.98	0.7	4.16	0.6	4.07	0.8	3.68	0.7	4.51	0.7
July	4.05	0.6	4.13	0.6	4.37	0.8	3.55	0.7	4.55	0.7
August			4.12	0.6	4.46	0.7	3.60	0.6	4.27	0.7
September			4.16	0.5	4.49	0.7	3.50	0.6	4.11	0.7
October			4.04	0.5	4.19	0.7	3.38	0.7	4.07	0.8
November			4.00	0.5	4.26	0.7	3.35	0.7	3.99	0.7
December			3.86	0.6	4.46	0.7	3.35	0.7	3.96	0.7
Annual Average	3.81	0.61	4.17	0.6	3.98	0.7	3.66	0.7	4.45	0.7

	2010 Rate	2010 Pts	2009 Rate	2009 Pts	2008 Rate	2008 Pts	2007 Rate	2007 Pts	2006 Rate	2006 Pts
January	5.03	0.7	5.05	0.7	5.76	0.4	6.22	0.4	6.15	0.5
February	4.99	0.7	5.13	0.7	5.92	0.5	6.29	0.4	6.25	0.6
March	4.97	0.7	5.00	0.7	5.97	0.5	6.16	0.4	6.32	0.6
April	5.10	0.7	4.81	0.7	5.92	0.4	6.18	0.5	6.51	0.6
May	4.89	0.7	4.86	0.7	6.04	0.5	6.26	0.4	6.60	0.5
June	4.74	0.7	5.42	0.7	6.32	0.7	6.66	0.4	6.68	0.5
July	4.56	0.7	5.22	0.7	6.43	0.6	6.70	0.4	6.76	0.5
August	4.43	0.7	5.19	0.7	6.48	0.7	6.57	0.4	6.52	0.4
September	4.35	0.7	5.06	0.7	6.04	0.7	6.38	0.5	6.40	0.5
October	4.23	0.8	4.95	0.7	6.20	0.6	6.38	0.5	6.36	0.4
November	4.30	0.8	4.88	0.7	6.09	0.7	6.21	0.4	6.24	0.5
December	4.71	0.7	4.93	0.7	5.29	0.7	6.10	0.5	6.14	0.4
Annual Average	4.69	0.7	5.04	0.7	6.03	0.6	6.34	0.4	6.41	0.5

	2005 Rate	2005 Pts	2004 Rate	2004 Pts	2003 Rate	2003 Pts	2002 Rate	2002 Pts	2001 Rate	2001 Pts
January	5.71	0.7	5.71	0.7	5.92	0.6	7	0.8	7.03	0.9
February	5.63	0.7	5.64	0.7	5.84	0.6	6.89	0.7	7.05	1
March	5.93	0.7	5.45	0.7	5.75	0.6	7.01	0.7	6.95	0.9
April	5.86	0.6	5.83	0.7	5.81	0.6	6.99	0.7	7.08	0.9
May	5.72	0.6	6.27	0.7	5.48	0.6	6.81	0.7	7.15	1
June	5.58	0.6	6.29	0.6	5.23	0.6	6.65	0.6	7.16	1
July	5.70	0.5	6.06	0.6	5.63	0.5	6.49	0.6	7.13	0.9
August	5.82	0.5	5.87	0.7	6.26	0.7	6.29	0.6	6.95	0.9
September	5.77	0.6	5.75	0.7	6.15	0.6	6.09	0.6	6.82	0.9
October	6.07	0.5	5.72	0.7	5.95	0.6	6.11	0.6	6.62	0.9
November	6.33	0.6	5.73	0.6	5.93	0.6	6.07	0.6	6.66	0.8
December	6.27	0.5	5.75	0.6	5.88	0.7	6.05	0.6	7.07	0.8
Annual Average	5.87	0.6	5.84	0.7	5.83	0.6	6.54	0.6	6.97	0.9

Compound Annual Returns for Ten-Year Holding Periods, % per year

Period	Common Stocks Large Company	Common Stocks Small Company	Long Term Corporate Bonds	Long Term Gov't. Bonds	Intermed. Gov't. Bonds	U.S. Treasury Bills	Inflation	Risk Premium	Small firm Premium
1926-1935	5.86	0.34	7.08	4.97	4.73	1.97	(2.57)	0.89	(5.52)
1927-1936	7.81	5.45	7.02	4.95	4.50	1.66	(2.30)	2.86	(2.36)
1928-1937	0.02	(5.22)	6.54	4.08	4.20	1.37	(1.80)	(4.06)	(5.24)
1929-1938	(0.89)	(5.70)	6.88	4.63	4.73	1.02	(1.98)	(5.52)	(4.81)
1930-1939	(0.05)	1.38	6.95	4.88	4.58	0.55	(2.05)	(4.93)	1.43
1931-1940	1.80	5.81	6.49	5.02	4.21	0.32	(1.34)	(3.22)	4.01
1932-1941	6.43	12.28	6.97	5.69	4.51	0.21	0.58	0.74	5.85
1933-1942	9.35	17.14	6.15	4.39	3.83	0.15	2.59	4.96	7.79
1934-1943	7.17	14.20	5.40	4.62	3.93	0.15	2.85	2.55	7.03
1935-1944	9.28	16.66	4.53	3.91	3.22	0.17	2.86	5.37	7.38
1936-1945	8.42	19.18	3.99	4.46	2.75	0.18	2.79	3.96	10.76
1937-1946	4.41	11.98	3.49	3.70	2.54	0.20	4.39	0.71	7.57
1938-1947	9.62	22.24	2.96	3.40	2.48	0.22	4.97	6.22	12.62
1939-1948	7.26	18.57	2.77	3.19	2.04	0.30	5.55	4.07	11.31
1940-1949	9.17	20.69	2.70	3.24	1.83	0.41	5.41	5.93	11.52
1941-1950	13.38	25.37	2.57	2.64	1.60	0.53	5.91	10.74	11.99
1942-1951	17.28	27.51	2.02	2.13	1.59	0.67	5.53	15.15	10.23
1943-1952	17.09	23.27	2.11	1.93	1.56	0.81	4.69	15.16	6.18
1944-1953	14.31	14.93	2.17	2.08	1.60	0.96	4.43	12.23	0.62
1945-1954	17.12	15.43	2.23	2.51	1.69	1.01	4.16	14.61	(1.69)
1946-1955	16.69	11.29	1.87	1.33	1.40	1.14	3.96	15.36	(5.40)
1947-1956	18.43	13.14	0.98	0.76	1.25	1.35	2.53	17.67	(5.29)
1948-1957	16.44	11.27	2.07	1.76	1.93	1.61	1.96	14.68	(5.17)
1949-1958	20.06	17.23	1.43	0.79	1.61	1.68	1.86	19.27	(2.83)
1950-1959	19.35	16.90	1.00	(0.07)	1.34	1.87	2.20	19.42	(2.45)
1951-1960	16.16	12.75	1.67	1.22	2.40	2.01	1.77	14.94	(3.41)
1952-1961	16.43	15.07	2.43	1.73	2.55	2.08	1.26	14.70	(1.36)
1953-1962	13.44	13.28	2.86	2.29	2.94	2.19	1.30	11.15	(0.16)
1954-1963	15.91	16.48	2.74	2.05	2.78	2.31	1.40	13.86	0.57
1955-1964	12.82	13.47	2.68	1.69	2.92	2.58	1.57	11.13	0.65
1956-1965	11.06	15.33	2.58	1.89	3.09	2.82	1.73	9.17	4.27
1957-1966	9.20	14.02	3.33	2.85	3.60	3.05	1.77	6.35	4.82
1958-1967	12.85	23.08	1.95	1.13	2.93	3.15	1.78	11.72	10.23
1959-1968	10.00	20.73	2.44	1.75	3.52	3.52	2.07	8.25	10.73
1960-1969	7.81	15.53	1.68	1.45	3.48	3.88	2.52	6.36	7.72
1961-1970	8.18	13.72	2.51	1.30	3.95	4.26	2.92	6.88	5.54
1962-1971	7.06	12.30	3.10	2.47	4.63	4.49	3.19	4.59	5.24
1963-1972	9.93	14.22	3.04	2.35	4.59	4.60	3.41	7.58	4.29
1964-1973	6.00	7.77	2.93	2.11	4.89	4.98	4.12	3.89	1.77
1965-1974	1.24	3.20	2.13	2.20	5.05	5.43	5.20	(0.96)	1.96
1966-1975	3.27	3.98	3.59	3.03	5.74	5.62	5.71	0.24	0.71
1967-1976	6.63	9.60	5.35	4.26	6.54	5.65	5.86	2.37	2.97
1968-1977	3.59	5.50	6.07	5.20	6.58	5.74	6.24	(1.61)	1.91
1969-1978	3.16	4.48	5.79	5.10	6.47	5.94	6.67	(1.94)	1.32
1970-1979	5.86	11.49	6.23	5.52	6.98	6.31	7.37	0.34	5.63
1971-1980	8.44	17.53	4.18	3.90	5.73	6.77	8.05	4.54	9.09
1972-1981	6.47	17.26	3.00	2.81	5.80	7.78	8.62	3.66	10.79
1973-1982	6.68	19.67	6.06	5.76	8.00	8.46	8.67	0.92	12.99
1974-1983	10.61	28.40	6.43	5.95	8.28	8.65	8.16	4.66	17.79
1975-1984	14.76	30.38	8.39	7.03	9.11	8.83	7.34	7.73	15.62
1976-1985	14.33	27.75	9.84	8.99	10.31	9.03	7.01	5.34	13.42
1977-1986	13.82	0.90	9.95	9.70	10.53	9.14	6.63	4.12	(12.92)
1978-1987	15.26	18.99	9.73	9.47	10.69	9.17	6.39	5.79	3.73
1979-1988	16.33	18.93	10.86	10.62	10.97	9.09	5.93	5.71	2.60
1980-1989	17.55	15.83	13.02	12.61	11.91	8.89	5.09	4.94	(1.72)
1981-1990	13.93	9.32	14.09	13.75	12.52	8.55	4.49	0.18	(4.61)
1982-1991	17.59	11.97	16.32	15.56	13.13	7.65	3.91	2.03	(5.62)
1983-1992	16.19	11.55	13.28	12.58	11.04	6.95	3.81	3.61	(4.64)
1984-1993	14.94	9.96	14.00	14.41	11.43	6.35	3.71	0.53	(4.98)
1985-1994	14.40	11.06	11.57	11.86	11.43	5.76	3.58	2.54	(3.34)
1986-1995	14.84	11.90	11.32	11.92	9.08	5.55	3.48	2.92	(2.94)
Average	10.70	13.75	5.34	4.75	5.17	3.73	3.61	**5.95**	**3.05**

The risk premium for equity is: (common stock yield) - (long term gov't. bond yield), average, 1926-1995.

The risk premium small firms is: (return for stocks, large firms) - (return for stocks, small firms).

Source: *Stocks, Bonds, Bills, and Inflation.* 1996 Yearbook. Chicago: Ibbotson Associates, 1996, p. 45.

Exhibit B

Santa Monica Ordinance, Short Term Rentals

May 12, 2015

ORDINANCE NUMBER 2484 (CCS)

(City Council Series)

AN ORDINANCE OF THE CITY COUNCIL OF THE CITY OF
SANTA MONICA ADDING CHAPTER 6.20 TO THE SANTA MONICA
MUNICIPAL CODE CLARIFYING PROHIBITIONS AGAINST VACATION RENTALS
AND IMPOSING REGULATIONS ON HOME SHARING

WHEREAS, the City consists of just eight square miles of coastal land which is home to 90,000 residents, the job site of 300,000 workers, and a destination for as many as 500,000 visitors on weekends and holidays; and

WHEREAS, Santa Monica's primary housing goals include preserving its housing stock and preserving the quality and character of its existing single and multi-family residential neighborhoods. Santa Monica's prosperity has always been fueled by the area's many attractive features including its cohesive and active residential neighborhoods and the diverse population which resides therein. In order to continue to flourish, the City must preserve its available housing stock and the character and charm which result, in part, from cultural, ethnic, and economic diversity of its resident population; and

WHEREAS, the City must also preserve its unique sense of community which derives, in large part, from residents' active participation in civic affairs, including local government, cultural events, and educational endeavors; and

1

WHEREAS, Santa Monica's natural beauty, its charming residential communities, its vibrant commercial quarters and its world class visitor serving amenities have drawn visitors from around the United States and around the world; and

WHEREAS, the City affords a diverse array of visitor-serving short term rentals, including, hotels, motels, bed and breakfasts, vacation rentals and home sharing, not all of which are currently authorized by local law; and

WHEREAS, operations of vacation rentals, where residents rent-out entire units to visitors and are not present during the visitors' stays are detrimental to the community's welfare and are prohibited by local law, because occupants of such vacation rentals, when not hosted, do not have any connections to the Santa Monica community and to the residential neighborhoods in which they are visiting; and

WHEREAS, the presence of such visitors within the City's residential neighborhoods can sometimes disrupt the quietude and residential character of the neighborhoods and adversely impact the community; and

WHEREAS, judicial decisions have upheld local governments' authority to prohibit vacation rentals; and

WHEREAS, with the recent advent of the so called "sharing economy," there is growing acceptance of the longstanding practice of "home-sharing," whereby residents host visitors in their homes for short periods of stay, for compensation, while the resident host remains present throughout the visitors' stay; and

2

WHEREAS, long before the advent of the sharing economy, home-sharing activities were already commonly undertaken throughout Santa Monica and throughout the United States; and

WHEREAS, history has shown that home-sharing activities spread the good-will of Santa Monica worldwide and have enhanced Santa Monica's image throughout the world; and

WHEREAS, home-sharing does not create the same adverse impacts as unsupervised vacation rentals because, among other things, the resident hosts are present to introduce their guests to the City's neighborhoods and regulate their guests' behavior; and

WHEREAS, history has shown that home-sharing activities are relatively very small in number, when compared to the number of persons utilizing vacation rentals or the City's hotels and motels; and

WHEREAS, while the City recognizes that home-sharing activities can be conducted in harmony with surrounding uses, those activities must be regulated to ensure that the small number of home-sharers stay in safe structures and do not threaten or harm the public health or welfare; and

WHEREAS, any monetary compensation paid to the resident hosts for their hospitality and hosting efforts rightfully belong to such hosts and existing law authorizes the City to collect Transient Occupancy Taxes ("TOTs") for vacation rentals and home-sharing activities; and

3

WHEREAS, existing law obligates both the hosts and rental agencies or hosting platforms to collect and remit TOTs to the City.

NOW, THEREFORE, THE CITY COUNCIL OF THE CITY OF SANTA MONICA DOES HEREBY ORDAIN AS FOLLOWS:

SECTION 1. Chapter 6.20 of the Santa Monica Municipal Code is hereby added to read as follows:

Chapter 6.20 HOME SHARING AND VACATION RENTALS

6.20.010   Definitions

For purposes of this Chapter, the following words or phrases shall have the following meanings:

(a)   Home-Sharing. An activity whereby the residents host visitors in their homes, for compensation, for periods of 30 consecutive days or less, while at least one of the dwelling unit's primary residents lives on-site, in the dwelling unit, throughout the visitors' stay.

(b)   Hosting Platform.   A marketplace in whatever form or format which facilitates the Home-Sharing or Vacation Rental, through advertising, match-making or any other means, using any medium of facilitation, and from which the operator of the hosting platform derives revenues, including booking fees or advertising revenues, from providing or maintaining the marketplace.

(c)   Vacation Rental. Rental of any dwelling unit, in whole or in part, within the City of Santa Monica, to any person(s) for exclusive transient use of 30 consecutive days or less, whereby the unit is only approved for permanent residential occupancy and not approved for transient occupancy or Home-Sharing as authorized by this

4

Chapter. Rental of units within City approved hotels, motels and bed and breakfasts shall not be considered Vacation Rental.

6.20.020   Home-Sharing Authorization

(a)   Notwithstanding any provision of this Code to the contrary, Home-Sharing shall be authorized in the City, provided that the Home-Sharing host complies with each of the following requirements:

(1)   Obtains and maintains at all times a City Business License authorizing Home-Sharing activity.

(2)   Operates the Home-Sharing activity in compliance with all Business License permit conditions, which may be imposed by the City to effectuate the purpose of this Chapter.

(3)   Collects and remits Transient Occupancy Tax ("TOT"), in coordination with any Hosting Platform if utilized, to the City and complies with all City TOT requirements as set forth in Chapter 6.68 of this Code.

(4)   Takes responsibility for and actively prevents any nuisance activities that may take place as a result of Home-Sharing activities.

(5)   Complies with all applicable laws, including all health, safety, building, fire protection, and rent control laws.

(6)   Complies with the regulations promulgated pursuant to this Chapter.

(b)   If any provision of this Chapter conflicts with any provision of the Zoning Ordinance codified in Article IX of this Code, the terms of this Chapter shall prevail.

5

6.20.030   Prohibitions

(a)   No person, including any Hosting Platform operator, shall undertake, maintain, authorize, aid, facilitate or advertise any Home-Sharing activity that does not comply with Section 6.20.020 of this Code or any Vacation Rental activity.

6.20.050   Hosting Platform Responsibilities

The operator / owner of any Hosting Platform shall:

(a)   be responsible for collecting all applicable TOTs and remitting the same to the City. The Hosting Platform shall be considered an agent of the host for purposes of TOT collections and remittance responsibilities as set forth in Chapter 6.68 of this Code.

(b)   disclose to the City on a regular basis each Home Sharing and Vacation Rental listing located in the City, the names of the persons responsible for each such listing, the address of each such listing, the length of stay for each such listing and the price paid for each stay.

6.20.080   Regulations

The City Manager or his or her designee may promulgate regulations, which may include but are not limited to permit conditions, reporting requirements, inspection frequencies, enforcement procedures, advertising restrictions, disclosure requirements, or insurance requirements, to implement the provisions of this Chapter. No person shall fail to comply with any such regulation.

6.20.090   Fees

The City Council may establish and set by Resolution all fees and charges as may be necessary to effectuate the purpose of this Chapter.

6

6.20.100   Enforcement.

(a)   Any person violating any provision of this Chapter shall be guilty of an infraction, which shall be punishable by a fine not exceeding two hundred fifty dollars, or a misdemeanor, which shall be punishable by a fine not exceeding five hundred dollars, or by imprisonment in the County Jail for a period not exceeding six months or by both such fine and imprisonment.

(b)   Any person convicted of violating any provision of this Chapter in a criminal case or found to be in violation of this Chapter in a civil case brought by a law enforcement agency shall be ordered to reimburse the City and other participating law enforcement agencies their full investigative costs, pay all back TOTs, and remit all illegally obtained rental revenue to the City so that it may be returned to the Home-Sharing visitors or used to compensate victims of illegal short term rental activities.

(c)   Any person who violates any provision of this Chapter shall be subject to administrative fines and administrative penalties pursuant to Chapter 1.09 and Chapter 1.10 of this Code.

(d)   Any interested person may seek an injunction or other relief to prevent or remedy violations of this Chapter.   The prevailing party in such an action shall be entitled to recover reasonable costs and attorney's fees.

(e)   The remedies provided in this Section are not exclusive, and nothing in this Section shall preclude the use or application of any other remedies, penalties or procedures established by law.

7

SECTION 2. Any provision of the Santa Monica Municipal Code or appendices thereto inconsistent with the provisions of this Ordinance, to the extent of such inconsistencies and no further, is hereby repealed or modified to that extent necessary to effect the provisions of this Ordinance.

SECTION 3. If any section, subsection, sentence, clause, or phrase of this Ordinance is for any reason held to be invalid or unconstitutional by a decision of any court of competent jurisdiction, such decision shall not affect the validity of the remaining portions of this Ordinance. The City Council hereby declares that it would have passed this Ordinance and each and every section, subsection, sentence, clause, or phrase not declared invalid or unconstitutional without regard to whether any portion of the ordinance would be subsequently declared invalid or unconstitutional.

SECTION 4. The Mayor shall sign and the City Clerk shall attest to the passage of this Ordinance. The City Clerk shall cause the same to be published once in the official newspaper within 15 days after its adoption. This Ordinance shall become effective 30 days from its adoption.

APPROVED AS TO FORM:

MARSHA JONES MOUTRIE
City Attorney

8

Approved and adopted this 12th day of May, 2015.

Kevin McKeown, Mayor

State of California   )
County of Los Angeles   ) ss.
City of Santa Monica   )

I, Sarah P. Gorman, City Clerk of the City of Santa Monica, do hereby certify that the foregoing Ordinance No. 2484 (CCS) had its introduction on April 28, 2015, and was adopted at the Santa Monica City Council meeting held on May 12, 2015, by the following vote:

Ayes: Councilmembers: Davis, Himmelrich, O'Connor, O'Day, Winterer
                                        Mayor McKeown, Mayor Pro Tem Vazquez

Noes: Councilmembers: None

Absent: Councilmembers: None

A summary of Ordinance No. 2484 (CCS) was duly published pursuant to California Government Code Section 40806 .

ATTEST:

Sarah P. Gorman, City Clerk

Exhibit C

California Senate Bill, SB 593

April 6, 2015

AMENDED IN SENATE JUNE 10, 2015

AMENDED IN SENATE MAY 6, 2015

AMENDED IN SENATE APRIL 29, 2015

AMENDED IN SENATE APRIL 6, 2015

SENATE BILL   No. 593

Introduced by Senator McGuire
(Coauthor: Senator Leno)

February 27, 2015

An act to add Article 12 (commencing with Section53170) to Chapter 1 of Part 1 of Division 2 of Title 5 of the Government Code, relating to local government.

LEGISLATIVE COUNSEL'S DIGEST

SB 593, as amended, McGuire. Residential units for tourist or transient use: *transient residential* hosting platforms.

The California Constitution authorizes a county or city to make and enforce within its limits all local, police, sanitary, and other ordinances and regulations not in conflict with general laws. *Existing law also authorizes a city, county, or city and county to impose a transient occupancy tax upon occupancies of lodgings of no more than 30 days.*

~~This bill would require an operator of a hosting platform, as defined, to report specified information quarterly to the city, county, or city and county. The bill would authorize a city, county, or city and county, by ordinance, to opt out from receiving reports and to subsequently opt back in, with 90 days' advance notice of that ordinance to the operator of a hosting platform and to impose a fine or penalty on an operator that fails to provide the report, as specified. The bill would prohibit an operator of a hosting platform from facilitating the rental of a residential~~

unit offered for occupancy for tourist or transient use, if such a use of ~~that residential unit, or the offering of that residential unit for such a use,~~ ~~is prohibited by an ordinance of the city, county, or city and county in~~ ~~which that residential unit is located. The bill would authorize a city,~~ ~~county, or city and county, by ordinance, to establish a fine or penalty on~~ ~~an operator of a hosting platform, as specified, for a knowing violation~~ ~~of this provision. The bill would authorize a city, county, or city and~~ ~~county to require an operator of a hosting platform to collect and remit~~ ~~applicable local transient occupancy tax.~~

This bill would authorize a city, county, or city and county to adopt an ordinance that would require a transient residential hosting platform, as defined, to report specified information quarterly to the city, county, or city and county, and to establish, by ordinance, a fine or penalty on a transient residential hosting platform for failure to provide the report. The bill would make the information in the report confidential and require that it not be disclosed. The bill would authorize the city, county, or city and county receiving the report to use the report solely for transient occupancy tax and zoning administration. The bill would also authorize a city, county, or city and county to require a transient residential hosting platform to collect and remit applicable transient occupancy tax.

The bill, where a specified ordinance has been adopted, would prohibit a transient residential hosting platform from facilitating occupancy of a residential unit offered for tourist or transient use in violation of any ordinance, regulation, or law of the city, county, or city and county, and would authorize a city, county, or city and county, by ordinance, to establish a civil fine or penalty on an operator of a transient residential hosting platform for a knowing violation of this provision.

This bill would also require the operator of a transient residential hosting platform to disclose specified information regarding insurance coverage in the transient residential hosting platform agreement with an offeror of a residential unit.

Existing constitutional provisions require that a statute that limits the right of access to the meetings of public bodies or the writings of public officials and agencies be adopted with findings demonstrating the interest protected by the limitation and the need for protecting that interest.

This bill would make legislative findings to that effect.

The California Constitution requires local agencies, for the purpose of ensuring public access to the meetings of public bodies and the writings of public officials and agencies, to comply with a statutory enactment that amends or enacts laws relating to public records or open meetings and contains findings demonstrating that the enactment furthers the constitutional requirements relating to this purpose.
This bill would make legislative findings to that effect.

Vote: majority. Appropriation: no. Fiscal committee: no.
State-mandated local program: no.

The people of the State of California do enact as follows:
1   SECTION 1.   Article 12 (commencing with Section 53170) is
2 added to Chapter 1 of Part 1 of Division 2 of Title 5 of the
3 Government Code, to read:
4
5   Article 12. Thriving Communities and Sharing Economy Act
6
7   53170. *(a)* This article shall be known, and may be cited, as
8 the Thriving Communities and Sharing Economy Act.
9   *(b) The Legislature finds and declares that transient residential*
10 *hosting platforms are doing business in California by facilitating*
11 *the occupancy of property located in California.*
12 53171. ~~(a)~~ For purposes of this article:
13 ~~(1) "Hosting~~
14 *(a) (1) "Transient residential hosting* platform" means ~~a~~
15 ~~marketplace that is created for the primary purpose of facilitating~~
16 *a person or entity that facilitates* the rental of a residential unit
17 offered for occupancy for tourist or transient use for compensation
18 to the offeror of that unit, and the ~~operator of the~~ *transient*
19 *residential* hosting platform derives revenues, including booking
20 ~~fees~~ *fees, subscription charges,* or advertising ~~revenues, from~~
21 ~~providing or maintaining that marketplace. "Facilitating"~~ *revenues.*
22 *"Facilitate"* includes, but is not limited to, the act of allowing the
23 offeror of the residential unit to offer or advertise the residential
24 unit on the Internet Web site provided or maintained by the
25 operator.
26 *(2) "Transient residential hosting platform" does not include*
27 *anyone licensed to practice real estate as defined in Section 10130*
28 *of the Business and Professions Code.*

111

1　(2)

2　*(b)* "Offeror" ~~includes an owner or lessee~~ *means the owner,*
3　*lessee, or other person or entity with the legal right to occupy or*
4　*authorize the occupancy* of a residential unit.

5　(3)

6　*(c)* "Residential unit" means a dwelling unit in a private
7　residence, including a single-family residence, an apartment or
8　other leased premises, a residential condominium unit, or any other
9　residential real estate improvement. "Residential unit" does not
10　include individual guest ~~rooms, condominium units, timeshare~~
11　~~units, cabins, or similar guest accommodations rented to transient~~
12　~~guests~~ *rooms* in a hotel, inn, or similar transient lodging
13　establishment operated by an innkeeper, as defined in subdivision
14　(a) of Section 1865 of the Civil Code.

15　*(d) "Tourist or transient use" means 30 days or fewer.*

16　*(e) "Operator" includes any corporation, partnership, or*
17　*individual that provides or maintains a transient residential hosting*
18　*platform.*

19　~~(b) (1) Except as provided in paragraph (2), the operator of a~~

20　*53172. All of the following shall apply only within the*
21　*jurisdiction of a city, county, or city and county that adopts an*
22　*ordinance applying this section within its jurisdiction:*

23　*(a) A transient residential* hosting platform shall report quarterly
24　to the city, county, or city and county all of the following
25　information:

26　(A)

27　*(1)* The address of each residential unit that was ~~offered on the~~
28　~~operator's hosting platform for occupancy for tourist or transient~~
29　~~use and was occupied for that use~~ *occupied for tourist or transient*
30　*use* during that quarterly period.

31　(B)

32　*(2)* The total number of nights that the residential unit was
33　occupied for tourist or transient use.

34　(C)

35　*(3)* The amounts paid for the occupancy of that residential ~~unit.~~
36　*unit for tourist or transient use.*

37　~~(2) A city, county, or city and county may, by ordinance, opt~~
38　~~out from receiving reports from an operator of a hosting platform~~
39　~~under paragraph (1) at any time and, subsequently, may, by~~
40　~~ordinance, opt back in to receive the reports. A city, county, or~~

95

112

1 ~~city and county shall provide the operator of a hosting platform~~
2 ~~with 90 days' advance notice of an ordinance adopted under this~~
3 ~~paragraph.~~
4 ~~(3)~~
5 *(b)* A city, county, or city and county may, by ordinance,
6 establish a fine or penalty on ~~an operator of a~~ *a transient residential*
7 hosting platform that fails to provide a report required pursuant to
8 this ~~subdivision~~ *section* not to exceed the amount of one thousand
9 dollars ($1,000) for the first failure, two thousand dollars ($2,000)
10 for the second failure, and five thousand dollars ($5,000) for a
11 third or subsequent failure, to be imposed after the city, county,
12 or city and county has provided written notice to the operator of
13 the failure, has given the ~~operator~~ *transient residential hosting*
14 *platform* an opportunity to provide the report within 30 days of
15 receiving the written notice, and the ~~operator~~ *transient residential*
16 *hosting platform* failed to provide the report within that period.
17 ~~(4)~~
18 *(c)* Any civil fines or penalties shall be paid to the city, county,
19 or city and county that established the fine or penalty.
20 ~~(e) (1) An operator of a~~
21 *(d) (1) Notwithstanding any other law, including the California*
22 *Public Records Act, as set forth in Chapter 3.5 (commencing with*
23 *Section 6250) of Division 7 of Title 1, the information in the report*
24 *required pursuant to this subdivision is confidential and shall not*
25 *be disclosed.*
26 *(2) The city, county, or city and county receiving the report*
27 *shall use the information in the report solely for the administration*
28 *of transient occupancy tax and zoning.*
29 *(e) The city, county, or city and county may require a transient*
30 *residential hosting platform to collect the transient occupancy tax*
31 *imposed by that local agency, and to remit that tax to that agency.*
32 *The authority granted by this subdivision is in addition to any*
33 *other provision of state or local law that authorizes a city, county,*
34 *or city and county to require a transient residential hosting*
35 *platform or any other person or entity to collect and remit transient*
36 *occupancy tax.*
37 *53173. (a) A transient residential* hosting platform shall not
38 facilitate the ~~rental~~ *occupancy* of a residential unit offered for
39 occupancy for tourist or transient use if ~~such a use of that~~
40 ~~residential unit, or the offering of that residential unit for such a~~95

113

1 ~~use, is prohibited by an ordinance~~ *the occupancy will violate any*
2 *ordinance, regulation, or law* of the city, county, or city and ~~county~~
3 *county,* in which that residential unit is ~~located.~~ *located, that has*
4 *applied Section 53172 within its jurisdiction.*
5 ~~(2)~~
6 *(b)* A city, county, or city and county *that has applied Section*
7 *53172 within its jurisdiction* may, by ordinance, establish a civil
8 fine or penalty on an operator of a *transient residential* hosting
9 platform that knowingly violates this ~~subdivision~~ *section* not to
10 exceed the amount of one thousand dollars ($1,000) per day for
11 the first violation, two thousand dollars ($2,000) per day for a
12 second violation, and five thousand dollars ($5,000) per day for a
13 third or subsequent ~~violation. An operator of a hosting platform~~
14 ~~shall be deemed to have knowingly violated this subdivision if a~~
15 ~~city, county, or city and county has previously provided the~~
16 ~~operator with a copy, including a copy in electronic form, of its~~
17 ~~ordinance prohibiting the use of a residential unit located within~~
18 ~~its boundaries for occupancy for tourist or transient use, or the~~
19 ~~offering of that unit for such a use, has given written notice of a~~
20 ~~known violation to the operator, has given the operator an~~
21 ~~opportunity to cease facilitating the rental of that residential unit~~
22 ~~within 30 days of receiving the written notice, and the operator~~
23 ~~failed to cease within that period.~~ *violation to be imposed after the*
24 *city, county, or city and county has provided written notice to the*
25 *operator of a transient residential hosting platform of the failure*
26 *to abide by the respective ordinance, has given the operator of the*
27 *transient residential hosting platform an opportunity to correct*
28 *the violation within 30 days of receiving the written notice, and*
29 *the operator of the transient residential hosting platform failed to*
30 *correct the violation within that period.*
31 ~~(3)~~
32 *(c)* Any civil fines or penalties shall be paid to the city, county,
33 or city and county that established the fine or penalty.
34 ~~(d) A city, county, or city and county may require the operator~~
35 ~~of a hosting platform to collect applicable transient occupancy tax~~
36 ~~imposed by that local agency, and to remit that tax to that agency.~~
37 *53174. An operator of a transient residential hosting platform*
38 *shall disclose the following in the transient residential hosting*
39 *platform agreement with an offeror:*

1 *(a) That an offeror should review his or her home or renter's*
2 *insurance policy to ensure that there is appropriate insurance*
3 *coverage in the event that a person sustains an injury or loss on*
4 *the offeror's property, a person damages or causes loss to an*
5 *offeror's personal or real property, or a claim or lawsuit is made*
6 *against the offeror or otherwise arises out of activities related to*
7 *the transient residential hosting platform.*
8 *(b) If the operator of the transient residential hosting platform*
9 *provides insurance coverage, that the insurance coverage is*
10 *provided and the limits of liability. If the insurance provided by*
11 *the operator of the transient residential hosting platform is excess,*
12 *secondary, or contingent upon an offeror's home or rental*
13 *insurance, the operator of the transient residential hosting platform*
14 *shall explicitly explain to the offeror when the offeror's insurance*
15 *is primary or first in line to cover liabilities arising out of the*
16 *activities relating to the transient residential hosting platform.*
17 *53175. Nothing in this article shall be construed to preempt a*
18 *city, county, or city and county law regulating operators of*
19 *transient residential hosting platforms.*
20 *SEC. 2. The Legislature finds and declares that Section 1 of*
21 *this act, which adds Section 53172 to the Government Code,*
22 *imposes a limitation on the public's right of access to the meetings*
23 *of public bodies or the writings of public officials and agencies*
24 *within the meaning of Section 3 of Article I of the California*
25 *Constitution. Pursuant to that constitutional provision, the*
26 *Legislature makes the following findings to demonstrate the interest*
27 *protected by this limitation and the need for protecting that*
28 *interest:*
29 *Where a city, county, or city and county adopts an ordinance*
30 *applying Section 53172 of the Government Code within its*
31 *jurisdiction, in order to ensure that the information disclosed to*
32 *local public agencies in the reports required by Section 53172 of*
33 *the Government Code is not used for purposes other than the*
34 *limited public purposes specified in that section, it is necessary to*
35 *limit the disclosure of those reports.*
36 *SEC. 3. The Legislature finds and declares that Section 1 of*
37 *this act, which adds Section 53172 to the Government Code,*
38 *furthers, within the meaning of paragraph (7) of subdivision (b)*
39 *of Section 3 of Article I of the California Constitution, the purposes*
40 *of that constitutional section as it relates to the right of public*
95

1 *access to the meetings of local public bodies or the writings of*
2 *local public officials and local agencies. Pursuant to paragraph*
3 *(7) of subdivision (b) of Section 3 of Article I of the California*
4 *Constitution, the Legislature makes the following findings:*
5 *If a city, county, or city and county adopts an ordinance applying*
6 *Section 53172 of the Government Code within its jurisdiction,*
7 *limiting disclosure of a record obtained by the local public agency*
8 *for purposes of tax and zoning administration furthers the purposes*
9 *of Section 3 of Article I of the California Constitution by*
10 *appropriately balancing the interest in public disclosure with*
11 *ensuring that this information is not used for improper purposes.*

95

116

Exhibit D

Rental Revenue, Airbnb Hosts, Los Angeles County, 2015

Financial Results, Short-Term Rentals
Airbnb Listings, Los Angeles County

Revenue by City, past 12 months

	Past 12 Months Host Revenue	Occupancy Tax, if 14%	Fees earned by Airbnb
Los Angeles	$ 100,539,032	$ 14,075,464	$ 145,363
Santa Monica	**17,463,927**	**2,444,950**	**22,090**
West Hollywood	6,049,197	846,888	5,888
Beverly Hills	4,062,032	568,684	3,250
Long Beach	3,995,515	559,372	8,411
Pasadena	3,084,743	431,864	3,985
Hermosa Beach	1,879,183	263,086	2,310
Culver City	1,575,104	220,515	2,344
Redondo Beach	1,516,891	212,365	2,214
Burbank	1,179,909	165,187	1,769
Glendale	1,041,734	145,843	1,414
El Segundo	446,604	62,525	1,157
Inglewood	426,851	59,759	677
Alhambra	383,629	53,708	787
Agoura Hills	326,813	45,754	660
Torrance	312,136	43,699	938
South Pasadena	297,289	41,620	446
Rancho Palos Verdes	273,094	38,233	659
Palos Verdes Peninsu	247,431	34,640	245
Arcadia	199,992	27,999	318
Claremont	181,977	25,477	374
Calabasas	172,301	24,122	195
San Gabriel	169,060	23,668	345
La Canada Flintridge	141,539	19,815	303
San Marino	133,516	18,692	66
Carson	128,360	17,970	321
Gardena	124,058	17,368	545
Cerritos	122,183	17,106	82
Monrovia	115,325	16,146	165
Pico Rivera	113,949	15,953	577
Whittier	112,682	15,775	253
Santa Clarita	110,561	15,479	165
Sierra Madre	93,699	13,118	110
West Covina	77,483	10,848	84
Walnut	76,311	10,684	106
Avalon	75,518	10,573	71
Rosemead	70,704	9,899	208
Pomona	61,682	8,635	316

Financial Results, Short-Term Rentals
Airbnb Listings, Los Angeles County

Revenue by City, past 12 months

	Past 12 Months Host Revenue	Occupancy Tax, if 14%	Fees earned by Airbnb
San Dimas	57,018	7,983	49
Signal Hill	56,645	7,930	235
Temple City	55,217	7,730	81
Palmdale	53,920	7,549	34
El Monte	51,285	7,180	136
Downey	47,380	6,633	172
Covina	45,083	6,312	104
Diamond Bar	38,874	5,442	74
Duarte	33,290	4,661	122
Montebello	23,469	3,286	83
San Fernando	22,135	3,099	18
Westlake Village	21,604	3,025	30
Bell Gardens	19,561	2,739	80
Glendora	18,588	2,602	63
Huntington Park	15,568	2,180	42
Azusa	13,927	1,950	33
Santa Fe Springs	9,583	1,342	68
Bellflower	7,083	992	18
Baldwin Park	5,931	830	8
Compton	1,890	265	2
South El Monte	666	93	3
Total	**$147,980,731**	**$20,717,302**	**210,666**

Financial Results, Short-Term Rentals
Airbnb Listings, Los Angeles County

Total Revenue, per month, 2015

	Jan	Feb	Mar	Apr	May
Los Angeles	$ 7,108,130	$ 6,939,284	$ 8,140,414	$ 6,665,192	$ 10,975,068
Santa Monica	**1,098,442**	**1,082,286**	**1,454,894**	**1,561,257**	**1,783,180**
West Hollywood	527,965	437,550	527,449	378,686	551,168
Beverly Hills	226,956	328,619	279,224	286,938	422,111
Long Beach	228,283	235,416	270,192	277,817	461,676
Pasadena	209,866	215,339	270,819	215,993	354,852
Hermosa Beach	86,763	113,374	121,671	146,498	188,025
Culver City	99,310	97,498	125,948	97,394	150,241
Redondo Beach	77,302	72,750	101,193	102,850	166,998
Burbank	62,807	72,619	83,966	119,639	149,125
Glendale	69,874	63,202	84,795	75,059	100,379
El Segundo	38,246	20,013	32,474	31,604	38,114
Inglewood	27,377	24,315	37,219	33,955	58,169
Alhambra	20,532	25,362	28,224	30,179	51,922
Agoura Hills	12,938	15,756	19,237	31,531	44,752
Torrance	18,805	11,545	17,045	24,667	30,516
South Pasadena	14,891	16,868	18,808	16,689	30,417
Rancho Palos Verc	6,084	7,828	19,440	14,480	18,783
Palos Verdes Penii	17,202	20,848	20,807	24,359	28,059
Arcadia	9,125	6,020	16,458	12,393	30,041
Claremont	4,023	11,416	12,364	14,889	39,623
Calabasas	7,522	10,133	4,280	14,579	28,608
San Gabriel	6,684	15,294	13,295	8,092	22,393
La Canada Flintric	10,354	1,709	8,310	9,244	5,667
San Marino	3,980	16,143	3,637	3,606	3,705
Carson	5,830	7,911	13,877	11,074	8,198
Gardena	6,235	8,034	7,815	12,216	15,361
Cerritos	34,140	2,640	1,790	4,338	13,874
Monrovia	7,734	7,763	9,684	6,428	14,818
Pico Rivera	5,579	5,586	10,480	6,058	11,661
Whittier	5,162	3,749	5,791	9,148	3,889
Santa Clarita	10,198	6,270	5,715	15,094	13,935
Sierra Madre	8,548	2,942	1,489	3,805	6,214
West Covina	676	5,783	2,265	3,985	9,095
Walnut	451	15,335	8,121	2,329	16,139
Avalon		4,083	3,620	25,839	9,458
Rosemead	3,758	2,986	6,143	3,929	6,385
Pomona	2,850	4,594	4,078	7,078	6,636

Financial Results, Short-Term Rentals
Airbnb Listings, Los Angeles County

Total Revenue, per month, 2015

	Jan	Feb	Mar	Apr	May
San Dimas	5,385	6,100	473	2,668	2,645
Signal Hill	3,360	3,900	5,270	5,070	3,500
Temple City	5,120	4,284	5,137	4,259	11,194
Palmdale		3,985	3,355	1,230	1,100
El Monte	1,220	2,962	7,621	1,642	5,077
Downey	4,089	2,490	2,010	4,579	4,547
Covina	2,280	2,782	1,628	11,144	5,132
Diamond Bar		1,849	2,895	1,744	7,570
Duarte	2,085	187	1,801	2,737	4,651
Montebello	8,053	480	3,020	480	960
San Fernando			235	3,140	2,445
Westlake Village	553	416	981	852	6,849
Bell Gardens	2,157	523	808	649	2,189
Glendora	750	780	2,125	1,580	1,470
Huntington Park	110	549		5,755	436
Azusa		196	405	3,464	1,183
Santa Fe Springs	891	784	850	512	70
Bellflower			49	343	2,090
Baldwin Park			785		
Compton			1,510		
South El Monte	-	-	153	-	-
Total	**$10,120,675**	**$9,971,130**	**$11,834,142**	**$10,360,759**	**$15,932,363**
Growth rate, %		**-1.5%**	**18.7%**	**-12.5%**	**53.8%**

121

Financial Results, Short-Term Rentals
Airbnb Listings, Los Angeles County

Total Revenue, per month, 2015

	Jun	Jul	TOTAL 7 mo, 2015	Price per night	Median stay, days
Los Angeles	$ 12,662,708	$ 12,998,151	$ 65,488,947	$ 133	5
Santa Monica	**1,914,580**	**2,142,824**	**11,037,463**	173	5
West Hollywood	640,115	749,449	3,812,382	198	5
Beverly Hills	421,871	639,410	2,605,129	216	6
Long Beach	484,775	530,695	2,488,854	109	4
Pasadena	336,004	425,137	2,028,010	131	6
Hermosa Beach	256,655	342,927	1,255,913	199	4
Culver City	190,732	172,651	933,774	123	5
Redondo Beach	211,514	276,996	1,009,603	135	5
Burbank	154,568	131,632	774,356	99	7
Glendale	146,245	125,846	665,400	111	7
El Segundo	69,592	70,750	300,793	102	4
Inglewood	62,306	43,854	287,195	68	9
Alhambra	45,021	40,187	241,427	75	7
Agoura Hills	30,134	34,971	189,319	154	3
Torrance	48,276	58,587	209,441	64	5
South Pasadena	41,277	42,364	181,314	120	6
Rancho Palos Verdes	50,085	54,643	171,343	143	3
Palos Verdes Peninsu	34,033	33,110	178,418	161	6
Arcadia	53,162	45,485	172,684	100	6
Claremont	34,399	17,204	133,918	164	3
Calabasas	16,944	44,187	126,253	158	6
San Gabriel	33,177	24,176	123,111	68	7
La Canada Flintridge	15,429	15,672	66,385	137	3
San Marino	9,425	10,365	50,861	290	7
Carson	23,020	11,440	81,350	73	5
Gardena	15,701	22,244	87,606	72	3
Cerritos	7,324	6,615	70,721	137	11
Monrovia	12,101	16,364	74,892	158	4
Pico Rivera	9,682	13,243	62,289	52	4
Whittier	29,458	17,053	74,250	100	4
Santa Clarita	9,535	8,940	69,687	90	7
Sierra Madre	3,594	11,444	38,036	134	6
West Covina	13,750	14,140	49,694	203	5
Walnut	4,519	8,317	55,211	114	6
Avalon	10,566	21,952	75,518	231	5
Rosemead	7,097	12,121	42,419	97	4
Pomona	6,594	14,395	46,225	56	3

Financial Results, Short-Term Rentals
Airbnb Listings, Los Angeles County

Total Revenue, per month, 2015

	Jun	Jul	TOTAL 7 mo, 2015	Price per night	Median stay, days
San Dimas	7,419	6,032	30,722	232	5
Signal Hill	4,994	4,951	31,045	85	3
Temple City	8,275	8,497	46,766	135	5
Palmdale	1,400	4,470	15,540	124	13
El Monte	7,306	11,276	37,104	66	6
Downey	6,840	7,352	31,907	60	5
Covina	4,832	2,375	30,173	65	7
Diamond Bar	11,011	6,180	31,249	129	4
Duarte	7,493	12,662	31,616	74	4
Montebello	1,025	970	14,988	68	4
San Fernando		3,605	9,425	153	8
Westlake Village	5,526	6,427	21,604	85	8
Bell Gardens	2,243	7,110	15,679	58	4
Glendora	6,608	4,440	17,753	59	5
Huntington Park	1,856	5,022	13,728	75	5
Azusa	4,885	1,666	11,799	66	6
Santa Fe Springs	971	1,522	5,600	38	4
Bellflower	1,276	1,610	5,368	53	7
Baldwin Park	880	1,551	3,216	56	13
Compton			1,510	57	17
South El Monte	-	238	391	67	3
Total	**$18,200,808**	**$19,347,497**	**$95,767,374**	**$ 114**	**5**
Growth rate, %	**14.2%**	**6.3%**			

Financial Results, Short-Term Rentals
Airbnb Listings, Los Angeles County

Active Listings, currently renting on Airbnb

	Entire Place	Private Room	Shared Room	Total Listings
Los Angeles	4,827	3,263	418	8,508
Santa Monica	**363**	**323**	**21**	**707**
West Hollywood	255	97	5	357
Beverly Hills	200	93	10	303
Culver City	72	67	2	141
	5,717	**3,843**	**456**	**10,016**

Data source: Airdna.co
This data includes only Airbnb data. This data does not include revenue
for other internet listing firms, such as HomeAway, One Fine Stay, or FlipKey.

The growth rate is the increase per month including seasonal variations.
The month-by-month growth does not show the long-term growth or trends.

The average, used as the central tendency for the price per stay, is the arithmetic mean.
The median, used as the central tendency for the stay, is the-mid point between high & low.

References

Suggested Sources for Additional Reading

Court Decisions

U.S. Supreme Court

Agins v. City of Tiburon, 447 U.S. 255 (1980)

Albrecht v. United States, 329 U.S. 599 (1947)

Chern v. Bank of America, 15 Cal.3d 866 (1976)

Chicago, B. & QR Co. v. Chicago, 166 U.S. 226 (1897)

Dolaan v. City of Tigard, 512 U.S. 374 (1994)

First Lutheran Church v. Los Angeles County, 482 U.S. 304 (1987)

Goldblatt v. Hempstead, 369 U.S. 590 (1962)

Kimball Laundry Co. v. United States, 338 US 1 (1949)

Lucas v. South Carolina Coastal Council, 505 US 1003 (1992)

Miller v. California, 413 US 15 (1973)

National Bd. of YMCA v. United States, 395 U.S. 85 (1969)

Nollan v. California Coastal Comm'n, 483 US 825 (1987)

Koontz v. St. Johns River Water Mgmt. Dist., 113 S.Ct 2586 (2013)

Los Angeles v. Patel, 135 S.Ct. 2443 (2015)

Moore v. East Cleveland, 431 U.S. 494 (1977)

Newark Morning Ledger Co. v. United States, 507 U.S. 546 (1993)

Palazzolo v. Rhode Island, 533 U.S. 606 (2001)

Penn Central Transp. Co. v. New York City, 438 US 104 (1978)

Pennsylvania Coal Co. v. Mahon, 260 U.S. 393 (1922)

Saia v. New York, 334 U.S. 558 (1948)

San Diego Gas & Elec. Co. v. San Diego, 450 U.S. 621 (1981)

United States v. Miller, 317 U.S. 369 (1943)

United States ex rel. TVA v. Powelson, 319 US 266 (1943)

Village of Euclid v. Ambler Realty Co., (1926) 272 US 365

Williamson County Reg. Planning Comm'n v. Hamilton Bank, 473 US 172 (1985)

Federal Court of Appeals

Arnett v. Myers, 281 F.3d 552 (6th Cir 2002)

City of Oakland, Cal. v. Hotels. com LP, 572 F.3d 958 (9th Cir 2009)

Coniston Corp. v. Village of Hoffman Estates, 844 F.2d 461 (7th Cir 1988)

Dodd v. Hood River County, 59 F.3d 852 (9th Cir. 1995)

Patel v. City of San Bernardino, 310 F.3d 1134 (9th Cir 2002)

Federal District Court

Burgess vs. Sherpherdstown (U.S. Dist Ct ND West Virginia, Dec. 21, 2012)

HomeAway Inc. v. San Francisco (U.S. Dist Court, ND Calif. 2015)

Mt Holly Citizens in Action, Inc. v. Township of Mount Holly (Dist Ct D NJ 2008)

Soroka v. Extended Stay, Inc. (Dist Ct ED Calif 2011)

California Supreme Court

Priceline. com Inc. v. City of Anaheim, 180 Cal.App.4th 1130 (2010)

Santa Monica Beach, Ltd. v. Superior Court, 19 Cal.4th 952 (1999)

Louis Stores, Inc. v. Dept. of Alcoholic Beverage Control, 57 Cal.2d 749 (1962)

People ex rel. Clancy v. Superior Court, 39 Cal.3d 740 (1985)

California Court of Appeals

In re Transient Occupancy Tax Cases, 225 Cal.App.4th 56, (2nd Dist 2014)

In re Transient Occupancy Tax Cases, Unpublished (2nd Dist 2012)

Ewing v. City of Carmel-By-The-Sea, 34 Cal.App.3d 1579 (6th Cir 1991)

Florida Circuit Court

Milo v. City of Venice, 2008 CA 552 SC (Dist Ct 12th Cir FL 2008).
   http://www.inversecondemnation.com/inversecondemnation/files/Milo_order_CA552SC_3_2008.pdf

Government Reports

Bosselman, Fred P., David L. Callies, and John S. Banta. *The taking issue: A study of the constitutional limits of governmental authority to regulate the use of privately-owned land without paying compensation to the owners.* Vol. 13. US Government Printing Office, 1973

Legal Treatises

Chemerinsky, Erwin, *Constitutional Law*, 4th Edition, Aspen Casebook. NY: Wolters Kluwer Law and Business, 2013.

Chemerinsky, Erwin, *Constitutional Law*, 2015 Supplement. NY: Wolters Kluwer Law and Business, 2015.

May, Christopher N., *Constitutional Law: National Power and Federalism*, 6th Edition, Wolters Kluwer Law and Business, 2013.

State Statutes, Codes, Ordinances, Manuals

Calif. Rev. & Tax. Code, Occupancy Taxes, Section 7280

Calif. Bus. & Prof. Code, Innkeepers, Sections 1861-1865

Florida Statute, An Act Relating to Public Lodging Establishments and Pubic Food Service Establishments, House Bill 883, 2011 *Fla. Laws* 119
http://laws.flrules.org/2011/119

Short Term Rental Ordinance, Santa Monica, CA ,Ordinance No. 2015-02, April 12, 2015 http://www.smgov.net/Departments/PCD/Permits/Short-Term-Rental-Home-Share-Ordinance/ Click on Santa Monica Municipal Code, Click on CodeAlert-Recently Enacted Ordinances.

Short Term Rental Ordinance, Flagler County Florida, Ordinance No. 2015-02, February 19, 2015

Transient Occupancy Tax, Chapter 13000*, County Tax Collectors Reference Manual,* California (2012*)*

Journal Articles

Adler, Jonathan H., Money or Nothing: The Adverse Environmental Consequences of Uncompensated Land Use Controls, 49 *Boston College Law Rev.* 301 (2008)

Bauman, Gus, The Supreme Court, Inverse Condemnation and the Fifth Amendment: Justice Brennan Confronts the Inevitable in Land Use Controls, 5 *Rutgers L.J.* 15 (1983-1984)

Been, Vicki and Joel C. Bauvais, The Global Fifth Amendment - NAFTA's Investment Protections and the Misguided Quest for an International Regulatory Takings Doctrine, 78 *N.Y.U. L. Rev.* 30 (2003)

Bosselman, Fred P., Property Rights in Land: New Statutory Approaches, 15 *Nat. Resources J.* 681 (1975)

Broussard, K., Social Consequences of Eminent Domain: Urban Revitalization against the Backdrop of the Takings Clause, 24 *Law & Psychol. Rev.* 99 (2000)

Callies, David L., Fred Bosselman and the Taking Issue. *Journal of Land Use & Environmental Law*, 3-10 (2001)

Christiano, Lawrence, Martin Eichenbaum & Sergio Rebelo, 2011. When Is the Government Spending Multiplier Large?, Journal of Political Economy, 119 *University of Chicago Press* 1 (2011)

Cogan, John F. & Tobias Cwik, John B. Taylor, & Volker Wieland, New Keynesian versus old Keynesian government spending multipliers, 34 *Journal of Economic Dynamics and Control 3* (2010)

Cusumano, Michael A., How Traditional Firms must Compete in the Sharing Economy, *Communications of the ACM*, 58,1, 32-34 (2015)

Dunham. Allison, Griggs v. Allegheny County in Perspective: Thirty Years of Supreme Court Expropriation Law, 1962 *The Supreme Court Review* 63-106 (1962)

Fee, John E., Unearthing the Denominator in Regulatory Taking Claims, 61 *The University of Chicago Law Review* 4 (Autumn, 1994)

Freyfogle, Eric T., The Owning and Taking of Sensitive Lands, 43 *UCLA L. Rev.* 77 (1995-1996)

Jefferson-Jones, Jamila, Airbnb and the Housing Segment of the Modern "Sharing Economy": Are Short-Term Rental Restrictions an Unconstitutional Taking? 42 *Hastings Const. L.Q.* 557 (2014-2015)

Jefferson-Jones, Jamila, Can Short-Term Rental Arrangements Increase Home Values? A Case for AirBNB and Other Home Sharing Arrangements, 13 *Cornell Real Estate Review* 1 (2015)

Hough, Charles M., Due Process of Law: To-Day, 32 H*arvard Law Review* 3 (1919)

Karkkainen, Bradley C., The Police Power Revisited: Phantom Incorporation and the Roots of the Takings Muddle, 90 *Minnesota Law Review* (2006)

Kaplan, Roberta A. & Michael L. Nadler, Airbnb: A Case Study in Occupancy Regulation and Taxation, 82 *U Chi L Rev Dialogue* 103 (2015).

Krauss, Josh. The Sharing Economy: How State and Local Goverments are Failing and Why We Need Congress to Get Involved, 44 *Southwestern Law Review* 365 (2015).

Merrill, Thomas W., Economics of Public Use, 72 *Cornell L. Rev.* 61 (1986-1987)

Miceli, Thomas J. & Kathleen Segerson, Regulatory Takings: When Should Compensation Be Paid? 23 *The Journal of Legal Studies* 2, 749-776 (Jun., 1994)

Michelman, Frank, Takings, 88 *Columbia Law Review* 8, 1600-1629 (Dec., 1988)

Nadler, Janice & Diamond, Shari Seidman, Government Takings of Private Property: Kelo and the Perfect Storm. *Public Opinion and Constitutional Controversy*, Nathaniel Persily, Jack Citrin, and Patrick Egan, eds., pp. 287-310, Northwestern Public Law Research Paper No. 07-05, *Oxford University Press* (2008)

Pindell, Ngai, Home Sweet Home? The Efficacy of Rental Restrictions to Promote Neighborhood Stability, 29 *St. Louis U. Pub. L. Rev.* 41 (2009)

Radford, R. S., *Why Rent Control is Still a Regulatory Taking*, The Radford Center for Law, History & Economics, Davis, CA, (2005)

Sax, Joseph L., Takings and the Police Power, 74 *The Yale Law Journal* 2 (1964)

Serkin, Christopher, The Meaning of Value: Assessing Just Compensation for Regulatory Takings. 99 *Northwestern University Law Review*, 677-742, (2005)

Stuart, Allyson Haynes, The Sharing Economy: How State and Local Governments Are Failing and Why We Need Congress to Get Involved, 44 *SW. L. Rev. 365* (2014)

Treanor, William M., The Origins and Original Significance of the Just Compensation Clause of the Fifth Amendment, 94 *The Yale Law Journal* 3, 694-716 (Jan., 1985)

Zervas, Georgios, Davide Proserpio, & John W. Byers, *The Rise of the Sharing Economy: Estimating the Impact of Airbnb on the Hotel Industry*, Boston Univ. School of Management Research Paper 2013-16 (Feb 12, 2014).

Ziegler, Edward H., Partial Taking Claims, Ownership Rights in Land and Urban Planning Practice: The Emerging Dichotomy between Uncompensated Regulation and Compensable Benefit Extraction Under the Fifth Amendment Takings Clause. 22 *Journal of Land, Resources & Environmental Law* 1 (2002)

Economic Data

The Budget and Economic Outlook: 2015 to 2025, Congressional Budget Office (CBO), January 26, 2015. https://www.cbo.gov/publication/49892

Consumer Price Index-All Urban Consumers, U.S. City Average, June 2014
http://www.gpo.gov/fdsys/pkg/ECONI-2015-07/pdf/ECONI-2015-07-Pg23.pdf

Economic Indicators, Council of Economic Advisors (CEO), August 2015.
http://www.gpo.gov/economicindicators

Economic Report of the President, Council of Economic Advisors (CEO), 2015.
https://www.whitehouse.gov/sites/default/files/docs/cea_2015_erp_complete.pdf

Gross Income, Short-Term Rentals, City of Santa Monica, 2015.
http://www.airdna.co

Interest Rate and Points on 30-Year Fixed-Rate Mortgages, July 2015
http://www.freddiemac.com/pmms/pmms30.htm

Monthly House Price Index for U.S., Federal Housing Finance Agency, 2015.
http://www.fhfa.gov/AboutUs/Reports/ReportDocuments/MonthlyHPIJuly072215.pdf

Selected Interest Rates (Weekly)-H.15, Board of Governors of the Federal Reserve System, 2015. http://www.federalreserve.gov/releases/h15/default.htm

Qualifications of the Author

The author, Richard R. Sylvester, J.D., Ph.D., is a mathematical economist, with focus on the valuation of privately-held companies, including intangible assets, partial interests, and contingent liabilities. For three decades, his biography has been published in Marquis' *Who's Who in the World* and *Who's Who in America*. He has been a featured lecturer at several national symposia, including a shared rostrum with former President Ford. He was the primary speaker for the June 27, 1991 ABC *Prime Time Live* documentary which was nominated for the Emmy.

As a staff advisor specializing in strategic planning, he has served major corporations for three decades, including General Motors, General Dynamics, Lockheed, TRW, and at Hughes Aircraft, where he was the staff advisor to Howard R. Hughes for commercial application of advanced technology. He has given presentations to the Science Advisor to the President, the Congressional Budget Office, the Council of Economic Advisors, and the Defense Science Board.

He has been selected by major law firms and the Board of Directors of Fortune 500 firms as an independent expert for issues involving strategic planning, acquisitions, turnarounds, initial public offerings, and valuation of intangible assets such as patents and music rights. Under contract with the U.S. Treasury Department, he analyzed international transfer pricing for integrated petroleum firms involving over $700 million in income tax. He valued the broadcast rights for the Perry Mason Show and the copyrights for science fiction writer Ray Bradbury. He has testified as an expert witness in economics and finance in Federal District Court and California Superior Court.

His education includes an M.B.A. from the USC, a J.D. from Loyola Law School, and a Ph.D. from UCLA in economics and management, with postdoctoral studies in power electronics. His competitive academic awards include grants from the Ford Foundation, General Motors, and the Federal Government. His university teaching experience includes UCLA, USC, Loyola University, University of Redlands, Pepperdine University, and California State University. He is the author of fourteen published books on federal law, mathematics and economics.

www.ingramcontent.com/pod-product-compliance
Lightning Source LLC
Chambersburg PA
CBHW050106220326
41598CB00043B/7400